THE WOMAN
IN INDIAN ART

THE IMAGE OF WOMAN

HEINZ MODE

THE WOMAN IN INDIAN ART

McGRAW-HILL
Book Company
NEW YORK

Translated from the German by Marianne Herzfeld,
revised by Professor D. Talbot Rice
We also want to thank Miss M. V. Downie for her assistance

CONTENTS

INTRODUCTION

Indian art is in many ways a discovery of the twentieth century. This is not to say that it was unknown earlier or quite disregarded. But it awakened interest only as an ethnological phenomenon, as one of the national peculiarities of India, and was thought of importance primarily as a curiosity, or even as a monstrosity. An interesting instance of this is the attitude of Goethe, who frequently mentioned in his poems that he regretted he was unable to love India as he might otherwise have done, because of his dislike of Indian sculpture.

In the late eighteenth and even all through the nineteenth century the outstanding works of Indian art were of course known in the West only from descriptions or very imperfect drawings, whereas a highly plastic art like that of India cannot be reproduced adequately by drawings. Even the art of the Greeks, whose sculptors are recognized as the greatest among the ancients, is more closely related to pictorial art than that of the Indians, and it is therefore not due to mere chance that the earlier non-photographic reproductions of their works are more satisfactory than those of works from India.

Nevertheless there were friends of Indian art in Germany even as early as the nineteenth century who praised it even though they did not know much about it. August Wilhelm von Schlegel for instance wrote his *Indische Bibliothek* because he loved India and wanted to set up its civilization as a model for that of other countries, but he had to use all the learning within his reach and a fair amount of romantic imagination in addition (1). At the same time one should, however, not overlook the fact that a great number of smaller works of Indian art, bronzes, ivories, even small sculptures of stone and particularly miniatures had come to Europe even earlier. But it is characteristic of this period that these works were not thought to be Indian. The miniatures were classified as Arabo-Persian and were included among the works of the Islamic world, while the small sculptures together with those of Chinese or Japanese origin were ascribed to Far Eastern Asia. The larger sculptures, many of them worked into the living rock or forming part of buildings, could not be moved from the place where they had been made. This is one of the great handicaps under which the general knowledge of Indian art has to labour, since only a small part of it can be made available for exhibition in museums. The individual figure forms part of a whole from which it can be severed only with difficulty—contrasting thereby with many of the works of ancient

Greek or Roman art. All this may help to explain why one may call Indian art a discovery of the present century thanks to its perfected photographic techniques, the growing passion for travel and the greatly improved travel-facilities. This is of course furthered by the general trend of art-appreciation, which has begun to break away from exclusive adherence to the tenets of classical art, a trend based on far-reaching changes in social life.

Indian art is a mirror of Indian femininity. Even a superficial observer will realize this when he looks at the subjects of the sculptures and paintings. One cannot fail to notice the large number of female figures or the pleasantly plump and charmingly feminine forms. This applies not only to the plastic arts and to painting, but also to literature. Here, too, Goethe's attitude must be mentioned—and this time full agreement may be expressed when he praises the description of the female figures in Indian poetry. Surely nowhere in the world than in India can women be better entitled to claim higher rank than men in art, whether through the quantity of representations, the quality of their execution or the importance of their symbolic content. Although the majority of Indian artists have been men, one could almost speak of Indian art as a "female" art, because all the three factors mentioned above apply here and serve to indicate its character.

It is therefore difficult to present a short survey of this subject without, on the one hand, becoming involved in sketching a general history of Indian art even if only in outline, or, on the other, omitting details of general importance by keeping too strictly to the chosen theme. Combining in her attitudes and her gestures natural beauty with the most refined achievements of civilization, the Indian woman symbolizes the Indian outlook upon life. This may be observed all through history from the small bronzes and terra-cottas of the Harappa civilization of the third and second millenniums B.C.—famed for the large number and sometimes also for the beauty of the female figures—to the works of modern times. The Indian way of representation is as foreign to the naturalistic or idealized art based on the Greek tradition as to the abstract art of the prehistoric European civilizations or the modern art of Western Europe, both of which have a tendency to create similar stylized formulae.

The naturalism of India stresses in the representation of women the well-developed and charming plumpness of the female body, its swelling surface, soft to the touch, and the grace of gestures which, although natural, are yet conditioned by civilizing influences. Wherever couples are shown it becomes obvious that the male figures adapt themselves to the females in a voluptuous naturalism, and in Western eyes might therefore appear not heroic but rather effeminate. Moreover it seems easier to conceive women than men as single figures, they can more easily be detached from the scenes in which they take part, acting as individuals and with a significance of their own.

Dancing is a characteristic of Indian art, and it is not by chance that it is closely related to the art of sculpture. There too femininity dominates the content of the art and the way its meaning and its specific beauty are shown, even when it is a man who organizes the dance or where dancing couples or larger groups are to be seen; there too the substance of the dance is concentrated on the female figure. The course of the dance is characterized by the inter-communion of the movements of the principal figure, to which corresponding gestures of one or several partners are added only occasionally from outside.

It is one step only from this statement of the "feminine" character of Indian art to that of its erotic content. One has to emphasize its general erotic aspect in spite of possible protests by people who cannot or will not see it, or at the risk of puritanical displeasure. Whatever its reason, the tendency to conceal this particular feature of Indian art has led to what may be termed a substitute terminology, which misrepresents the essence of the sexual-feminine spirit of the art, suggesting that this is determined exclusively by religious motives. Difficulties have been put in the way of outsiders, who have wished to have access to Indian works of art, by the assertion that only a thorough knowledge of Indian devoutness could enhance an understanding of the religious fervour evident in sculptures and paintings.

The basis of all the variations and shades of the Indian idea of femininity is formed by two contrasting philosophical concepts, the poles of which are kāma, sensuality, and moksha, liberation. It is typical of the Indian manner of thought that such a polarity forms a unity, the contradiction providing a means of approaching a higher unity with the help of these opposites. Naturally kāma is particularly suitable for representation in art, while moksha must be conceived as merely being present; though it is not shown in the picture, moksha stands

8

for a trait of greater depth, intended to further the understanding of the observer. This understanding can be of a religious as well as a philosophical character. It adds to the picture, which at first glance appears wholly sensual, a more profound value as a symbol. The representation of kāma therefore serves to awaken and to further the understanding of moksha.

Some Indian art historians are ashamed of the erotic art of their country. Even A. K. Coomaraswamy, the great pioneer of the history of art in India, has no real use for it. In his *History of Indian Art* he refers to the most outstanding monuments of this kind, the temples of Bhuvaneshvara, Konārak and Khajurāho in only a few lines, and what is more, he implies that Indian art had passed its zenith by the epoch to which they belong. Contrary to his opinion, Stella Kramrisch repeatedly insisted in her earlier writings that Indian art culminates in the representation of femininity. She also realized that the fusion of human and plant forms—for instance the motif of the embrace of trees, which will be mentioned later—was not intended as a realistic reproduction of anything that happened in nature, but rather as a symbol of the Indian conception of nature; it represents the amplification of a natural process by the creative artist (2).

It is high time to recognize that Indian art, and in particular Indian sculpture, does not need to be defended, excused or justified. Nobody can understand the language of Indian art who is confused by open or veiled narrow-mindedness or bigotry, or who allows its main subject and message only, as it were, a restricted space in the margin, and tries to palliate it shamefacedly. The essential contradiction which has perplexed many Indian art historians has its roots not in the art itself, but in the connection of art with life in India.

It is no secret that the Indian woman has unfortunately not always been held in as great an esteem in everyday life as in art. Nehru himself, who cannot be called prejudiced, had to admit that "the position of women in India was during many hundreds of years not a good one, neither according to law nor in public or social life" (3). For some time past there has been differentiation between the contradictory views on the legal and the social status of women expressed, on the one hand, in the *Dharmashāstras*, the textbook and law-codes of the classical period and on the other in the more liberal epic literature and the collections of stories. In literature the difficulty of discriminating clearly between art and life is ever present because even the more liberal literature frequently quotes from stricter ancient writings and therefore contains side by side contradictory views. It is often not easy to decide what gives a true picture of Indian everyday life. In contrast the message of the works of imagery is less equivocal and makes it possible to arrive at comprehensive conclusions.

The contradiction between the esteem in which women are shown to be held in works of art and their humble position in everyday life can be explained by the unbroken continuity of the thousands of years of Indian history. In the early ages of mankind the woman enjoyed a greater regard, socially as well as legally, than in later epochs. The ideological and cultural influence of the matriarchy of the epoch before the class system had been established was for a long time still felt in the patriarchal society with its division of classes; it served to fix the position of the woman according to her natural importance to society as mother, bearer and preserver of fertility and as the protector of the race. This strong social position of woman in early society, founded in her close relationship to nature, on fertility and on propagation, showed her to be the mother of the tribe and the common ancestress; somewhat later she was to become the goddess of fertility and the mother-goddess. In everyday life it made her the centre of the family, the keeper of the family's possessions; her work, her craftsmanship, and her artistic faculties became the respected mainstay of the life of the community, guaranteeing its permanence.

However, when the ancient Oriental states were founded and their superior civilization was evolved, man was already the decisive element in the family and in the state. The heaven of the gods also was now believed to be dominated by men, and in the conception of procreation the more important role was ascribed to the begetter, not to the childbearing woman. Though this constituted a more or less radical change, ideologically the traditional vital importance of the female element in society could not so easily be re-interpreted or concealed, and still less eliminated.

India is an example of a not too radical revolution. Its high civilization in early times, at Mohenjo Daro and Harappa, formed only an island surrounded by large tribal communities where men lived by farming or still even by hunting. Moreover this civilization eventually succumbed to the influence of the surrounding tribes, and so it happened that a lasting patriarchal civilization based on a class system was formed only by a second revolution, no earlier than the first millennium B.C. There still remain even today fairly large remnants of un-assimilated tribal cultures in India, which have to some extent hindered the development of Indian civilization, though they have also influenced it and have certainly in no small degree contributed to shaping the face of its civilization.

There has always been a marked contrast between the matriarchal conception based on tradition in large parts of the country, especially outside the small islands formed by the townships, and the patriarchal trend of India's civilization developed since 1000 B.C. In the plastic arts these earlier conceptions have been preserved in the most unadulterated form. In some respects one may therefore see there the true expression of the Indian nationality and the apex of the achievement of the original Indian civilization, an unbroken original force reaching from the earliest times of mankind to the present day. The outstanding characteristic of this art is feminine and erotic; to overlook or to deny this would mean completely to misunderstand Indian art.

It should be noted here that a parallel development was taking place with regard to popular art and that all that has been said above about Indian art and Indian literature applies in an even higher degree to Indian popular fairy-tales and popular poetry, to folk-dance, to folk-music, as well as to all figurative popular art and to the handicrafts. In all these spheres the position of woman, her authority, the esteem in which she is held, her co-operation and her share of responsibility differ considerably from the picture provided by the official reports or to be gauged from the study of the philosophical or the religious systems, from what we know of the life at the courts or in the towns, or the rules of the castes and the practices of the hermits. While art shows a refinement, a sublimation of ancient things, the works of popular culture often present pictures based on wishful thinking, that is on hopes of justice and of social well-being and prosperity; not by chance is this picture modelled on the idealized social conditions thought to have prevailed in earlier times.

India has often been called the original home of fairy-tales. And this for good reason: the unbroken tradition of Indian popular culture reaches farther back into the past than anywhere in Europe or in the Near East. Although it is not always easy to prove the derivation of individual fairy-tales, the logical consistency of this hypothesis, stated for the first time by the German Sanskrit scholar Benfey (1809—1881), cannot be doubted, and the motto so beloved by detectives, *chercher la femme*, can also be applied here (4). The woman is the heroine of the Indian fairy-tale; she may appear beautiful or clever, be possessed of magical faculties, or strive with courage to attain her goal; she may be lustful and not shrink from free-living, she may be shown as a goddess or a demon, as a snake-girl or a swan-maid, as queen or princess, but she can also take on the guise of a simple peasant girl or a modest housewife.

THE CELESTIAL WOMAN

Any study of the iconography of woman in Indian art has to distinguish between two main groups: one, the woman as celestial figure, goddess, demi-goddess, or demon, and two, the woman as earthly figure. In the earlier periods of Indian art the images belonging to the first group by far outnumbered those of the second, since the majority of Indian figures come from sacred buildings, whereas secular buildings with figurative decorations have been preserved only from comparatively recent epochs. Only miniatures, paintings on single sheets, and illustrations yield a considerable number of representations of secular themes; but these works are of fairly recent origin, as all of them belong to the time after A.D. 1000.

The proportion of the number of items in the two groups should, however, not be interpreted, as has frequently been done, as meaning that Indian art was almost completely a religious art. The literature of the first thousand years A.D. gives a reliable indication that secular art was flourishing then and that there were, for example, portraits and mural paintings in the palaces, and that there was, further, an art unrelated to the life at the courts, using a great variety of techniques; this too may be claimed to have been secular art (5). One has, however, to realize that in a civilization as homogeneous as that of India on the whole the changes from secular to sacred art were bound to fluctuate, as were also those from the art of the court to the art of the townsmen and of the peasants. Consequently images are to be found among the works of art in the temples which one would hardly have expected there, and which may be felt to be unseemly in such places, as for instance the secular stories depicted on early Buddhist buildings or the eroticism of the sculptures in the mediaeval Hindu temples.

On the other hand it is worth noting that religious themes were often used in secular art, and, as they formed a part of everyday occurrence, they were taken for granted by the Indian observer without inhibiting him at all or committing him to any special religious attitude. The distinction between the two main groups has therefore been made in this study chiefly to help in the understanding of Indian art. It is important not to include in the category of religious art anything which an Indian would regard as part of his homogeneous concept of Indian civilization and the world, whereas according to the European tradition in the history of art it would be called secular art. Moreover, distinctions based on the actual themes would hardly have significance in the classical Indian theory of art, since external criteria, like the rank and position of the patron or the place where the work was to be set up, would be afforded greater significance.

Bearing this in mind one may call the picture of a goddess symbolic, fixed as it is by the formal rules of a religious canon, though its subject displays the appearance of the goddess in the world of man. A large number of bodily attitudes and of expressive gestures of the limbs (bhangas and mudrās) may here be observed as well as three important groups of distinctive characteristics: first, the contemplative, quietly poised attitude (sāttva), second, the representative disposition emphasizing power and strength (rājas); and third, the lively temperament exhibiting the might and force of the goddess by her gestures which indicate destructive and bellicose activities (tāmas). The three postures, sitting, standing and moving, seem organically well adapted to these three "virtues and attitudes" (gunas).

It would be of no use to enumerate the Indian goddesses; their names alone would fill many pages, and in fact only a few of them are sufficiently outstanding to be looked upon as the focal point of the female pantheon.

Besides, many of the names of the great goddesses have hardly any bearing on their character, nor do they refer to more than a part of their qualities or some particular aspect.

Prominent among all is the goddess Durgā, known also as Pārvatī or Umā and often simply called the Great Goddess, Mahādevī. In her terrifying appearance she is known as Kālī, Cāmundā, and Candī; she is thought to be the wife of Shiva. She is undoubtedly one of the most ancient, pre-Aryan deities of India. She is sometimes represented as a beautiful and blooming woman, sometimes as a frightening slut. All the characteristic qualities of the original mother-deity are concentrated in her: femininity and fertility as well as destructive violence, charm as well as terrifying cruelty. She has been set up as the divine ruler of the animal kingdom; on occasions she is represented alone and worshipped in temples of her own, at other times along with her husband Shiva and the children of this marriage, Ganesha with the elephant's head, the god of wisdom, and Kārttikeya, the god of war, riding on a peacock. They are sometimes shown in pairs, sometimes in family-groups. Usually some animal (vāhana) is appropriated by her, either as a companion or as a beast on which she rides. On most of the extant images this is a lion, but it seems likely that originally a tiger

Durgā on a Tiger

stood in its place, or rather a tiger-like leopard, a detail which could connect the goddess with the most ancient forms of the mother-deity of Asia Minor, that is, with the sculptures of clay or stone from Hacillar and Chatal Huyuk, dating from the sixth millennium B.C. This could also explain certain representations of the female deity at Mohenjo Daro and Harappa. In the popular art of India this connection of the goddess with the tiger has been retained until now.

The next place among the goddesses, second only to that of Durgā may be claimed by Lakshmī, the wife of Vishnu; she too has a certain individuality. She is called Shrī, the goddess of fortune, and is said to have risen from the sea like Aphrodite. Kāma, the god of love, is her son; generally she is friendly and of a pleasing appearance. Although she achieved a more distinctly individual position than Durgā, she, too, may originally have been closely connected with the mother-goddess, may even have been identical with her. The third among the great goddesses is Sarasvatī, the wife of Brahma, whose appearance in art is clearer than that of her husband. She might originally have been a local river-deity, but later became the goddess of speech and learning, and was therefore particularly appreciated in literature. She alone seems to have had nothing in common with the original mother-deity.

Far behind these three deities follow the wives of other Indian gods, Indrānī or Aindrī, the wife of the ancient Aryan god-king Indra, or Savarnā, Svātī, and Mahā-vīryā, the wives of the sun-god Sūrya; only a few representations are known of these goddesses. There was, however, one pair of deities very popular in art, the river-goddesses Gangā and Yamunā. Gangā is supposed to be the daughter of Himavat, the Himālaya, and the sister of Umā (Durgā), while Yamunā was thought of as the daughter of the sun-god and the sister of Yama, the ruler of the realm of the dead. These latter two goddesses were frequently represented standing on their vāhanas, the tortoise and the crocodile-like makara, at each side of the gates of temples dating from the Gupta or later epochs. They were worshipped as personifications of the sacred rivers represented by them; they had to ward off disaster and to protect the temple (6).

Some local goddesses of whom representations are to be found fairly often could also be mentioned here, for example the snake-goddess Manasā, or Sītalā, the small-

pox-goddess mainly associated with Bengal, and Sashthī the goddess of child-birth, and many others. They, however, form part of the Indian pantheon of female deities, which has for thousands of years been rapidly increasing, in part by additions from more primitive civilizations.

Of prominent importance for art are numerous groups of divine beings or demi-gods; for example, there are those who live in trees (vrikshakās) or those who dwell as female demons in woods or on mountains (yakshinīs and rākshasīs) who are much dreaded as cannibals. To them belong also the apsarās and gandharvas, who hover or dance in the heavens of the gods, and the magic vidhyād-harīs, the bird-like kinnarīs, and the nāginīs, who resemble serpents. All of these belong to the escorts of great deities or mix with mankind as connecting links between the terrestrial and the celestial spheres. This makes them popular figures for scenes representing deities, where they are shown accompanying the chief personalities and are used to fill in empty spaces; this role accounts also for their popularity in epics.

Some of these groups seem to claim a more individual rank and greater freedom of worship. This applies in particular to the tree- and snake-goddesses on the one hand and to the group of female demons, the rākshasīs and yakshinīs, on the other. Figures like that of the above-mentioned snake-goddess Manasā are, as it were, personifications of snake-women; likewise the goddess Durgā, in her terrifying appearance as Kālī, has taken over traits of the female demons, for instance the canine teeth protruding from the corners of the mouth, the bulging eyeballs, the dishevelled hair resembling snakes, and other similar details. It seems that in particular the tree cult and the yaksha cults, but also the worship of snakes, date from the earliest times of Indian civilization; the more ancient of the higher religions, Theravāda-Buddhism and Jainism, favoured the absorption of this kind of cult, evidently because it enabled them to break through into the existing popular beliefs.

Two of these groups of figures achieve a genuine representation of man and thereby belong to secular art. At the stūpa railings and gateways of Bhārhut and Sānchī the yakshinīs are turned into beautiful protectors of the sanctuaries; they are conspicuous for their bewitching nudity and bareness just like the still more charming Indian dryads hanging among the branches of the trees, who also form part of the stone imagery of these buildings. In the same way the figure of a woman standing by a tree, surrounding its trunk with her legs as with tendrils and reaching with her arms into the foliage at the top, is widely used as a symbol in the representation of women. It represents, for example, the pregnant mother of Buddha, Queen Māyā, who gave birth to her child while standing at a tree in the Grove of Lumbini. Somewhat later it recurs in scenes showing the shepherd-god Krishna amidst beautiful shepherdesses; he himself sits in the tree while the young maidens look up and implore the thief of their garments to have mercy on them.

Some songs of India's classic literature describe maidens who make trees flower by touching them with their tender limbs, transferring, as it were, the function of bees to human beings; bees and lovely maidens are frequently used in Indian poetry as corresponding symbols. While all this evidently points to the ancient symbolism of fertility, it is also an eloquent example of the creative unity of the religious and the secular spheres of figurative art. In the early works of the Mathurā School, dating from the Kushāna period, the maidens standing at trees are represented in a definitely secular style so that the original theme of the images remains hidden to the present-day observer. Since then it has become part of whatever an artist wanted to do, to show scenes where lovely maidens are connected with trees.

Descendants of the yakshinīs and vrikshakās are the sūrasundarīs, heavenly beauties, whose images are often to be found on the outer walls of mediaeval Hindu temples; they are, as it were, used without any other motivation than to fill empty spaces in the sculptures, are pleasing to the eye, and offer the artist a chance of proving his ability in displaying overwhelming female charms. Here, too, the general idea related to the concept of feminity has influenced sacred art, though without adhering to any clearly defined or binding religion. The background remained that of purposeful sacred art, but otherwise

this is an instance of the fusion of the most ancient with quite modern views, forming the comprehensive basic rules of Indian art; in the introduction to this study it was termed "feminine"; it certainly is one of the most characteristic traits of Indian art.

It should perhaps be added that the figures of the principal women are often surrounded by dwarf-like figures suggesting children, though with regard to the subject of the scenes they might also be explained as ganas, that is, bands of dwarfs accompanying the gods. Side by side with the women appear also figures of feminized men, seldom alone and often as their partners, thereby enhancing the effect produced by the women themselves. It ought to be remembered that some of the great Indian deities appear as hermaphrodites, for instance Shiva as Ardhanārī, half man, half woman, and also Krishna, although the latter uses for his impersonation merely female attire, which he often favours.

The artistic value of the Indian representation of female deities is due to the originality of the designs and to the fact that their message was generally applicable to all works of outstanding quality. Of course some images are prevented from attaining any far-reaching effect, notably those works which the Indian believer, usually the Brahman acting as priestly mediator and ignoring the original intention of the artist, has hidden, or secreted by over-painting, or so clothed the figures that only some feature of the face looks out from a formless bundle. These represent endeavours to further a cult without images of any kind, where the mere presence of the deity is deemed sufficient, be it in a stone, in the form of a vessel, or in a formless bundle. Worship of that kind, though an important and interesting one from the religious point of view, is alien to the subject of this study.

THE TERRESTRIAL WOMAN

It is often difficult to distinguish the earthly woman from a deity, as is pointed out by the following form of address used in epic literature: "Are you a goddess? or a dānavī? a gandharva woman? an apsarās, a yaksha woman, a snake-fairy, or do you belong to the human race?" (7) At best there are some superficial means that aid identification which are provided by some of her attributes, by certain peculiarities of her garments, her jewelry or headdress, or by the scene associated with her. It is therefore not easy to classify the women of the human race who are represented in Indian art. Yet some attempt to do so may be made here on the basis of women's habits and activities, though it must be noted that working women are only rarely depicted in ancient or mediaeval art. Although the above-mentioned attributes cannot be taken as characteristics of any special goddess, there are some of a more general nature which serve to describe certain types of women or special moods of female beings.

To explain the different significance of the different attributes it may be best to point out the role which animals and plants play in this respect, both for some particular figure or something individual, on the one hand, and in respect of some general idea or mood on the other. The lotus, for example, with its wide-open or closed blossom, serves as the symbol of quite a number of deities. It either climbs upwards as tendrils to the right and left of the god and thus forms his seat, or it is held in the deity's hand. Often women too carry a lotus bud or an opened-up blossom, or they are placed amidst plants, a custom which is particularly favoured in miniature painting.

But here there is a different relation between the woman and the plant. In the first-mentioned group the deity has, as it were, chosen a special kind of plant to indicate her own character; in the second the plant characterizes by its appearance on the scene the mood or the emotions of the woman. Here the plant gives a special colouring to the general idea of femininity.

Similar particulars could be given of animal attributes. Some species of animal—bulls, buffaloes, elephants, and others—are used by special deities as vāhana (literally "vehicle") that is, in fact, as seats; they serve for riding or as animals forming an escort. Women may also be shown playing with a bird or chasing a cat, but this does not of necessity point to a special deity. Here the animal makes known the emotions of the woman, by leading her to amorous play, intimate conversation, or to angry outbursts. In the same way some of the activities of women are indicated in quite a general manner by certain objects. Jugs are carried on the head to denote the village-maid on her way to the well, a duster of palm-leaves or a household vessel are associated with servants, and a bowl filled with flowers indicates woman preparing to make an offering as part of her religious duties. These symbolic activities are rarely supplemented by more elaborate scenes, except on the narrative reliefs of the early Buddhist epoch and in the later miniature paintings.

THE WOMAN
AS MOTHER

The representation of woman in her most feminine function, childbearing or caring for the child, is one of the earliest types of image in the history of civilization. It forms an undercurrent to all periods of Indian history and appears to this day in popular art, in the art of the more primitive Indian tribes, and in the arts and crafts, frequently in a rigid idol-like shape. For this type of art the genetic connection with the original representation of the mother-goddess makes the distinction between religious and temporal subjects particularly difficult. Although in most of the instances no individual explanation can be given of the symbolic meaning of the single figure, this theme is generally thought to be not so much a realistic and therefore secular one, as to be possessed of a philosophical and, broadly speaking, a religious significance. In earlier Buddhist art the mother of Buddha personified the woman at childbirth; the same theme was symbolized by the mothers of Mahāvīra and of Krishna respectively in Jain or Vishnuite art, where they are shown as conceiving or giving birth either lying down or standing. The goddesses of one group, the so-called "Mothers" (mātrikās) are often characterized by the fact that they are holding a child in their arms.

In her quality as mother the woman was allotted an honourable place in society even in the period of the greatest Brahmanic predominance, though at that time it seemed important to stress the fact that she was the mother of a son. It was stated as early as in the *Mahābhārata* (about 400 B.C.) that the mother was the highest guru (spiritual teacher) of all gurus, and that there were means to avert and ward off all curses except a mother's curse, and that neither in this world nor in the wood of the ascetics was there any more noble religious exercise than that regarding the mother. "If one has a mother, one is secure, but insecure without her. He does not grieve, old age does not worry him who, even if betrayed by luck, can return to his home and say 'my little mother'. Be he surrounded by sons and grandsons, standing at the end of his hundredth year, when he flees to his mother he acts like a two-year-old child. Whether he is efficient or inefficient, the mother will protect her son, be he a man of consequence or insignificant; fate has given him no other guardian. Then he is old, then he is unhappy, then the world is empty and bare for him, when he is separated from his mother." (8)

17   *Woman on a Sofa with Child*

This esteem of the mother is also shown in language, as for instance in the Sanskrit composite word "mother and father" rather than "father and mother". In law, however, this high respect for the mother was contrasted by a low estimation of the woman. According to it the wife is the property of her husband. She alone is a wife whose husband is all her life; she alone is a wife who has borne children, is pure in thought, word, and deed and obeys the commands of her husband.

Notwithstanding the high significance of the subject, this group compared with others is of much less importance from the point of view of art. Again and again repetitions of closely related types of images are to be found which hardly tell anything about the everyday life of mother and child, except for the more detailed descriptions referring to the histories of the youth of Buddha or Krishna. The Indian artist has evidently been hindered by the traditionally fixed and comparatively simple symbolic mother-child figures; in addition to that, these representations suffer by their failure to reveal and display female charms, as if the artist wished to respect the sphere of the husband's or father's private property.

There are of course exceptions to be found on the walls of mediaeval Hindu temples, where a playful easing-off of the mother-child relationship can be observed and where the woman's body is again allowed to achieve the greatest effect as seen by the Indian idea of art. But some of these beautiful women, as they smile at their children or lift them up in their arms, seem to take a cheerful pleasure in playing, while the subject and meaning of this play eventually turns out to appear indifferent.

THE WOMAN
AS LOVER
AND BELOVED

Though this group of representations is also connected with the original image of the mother-deity, and though it is often difficult to distinguish between heavenly and earthly pairs of lovers, yet it is the most important group from the point of view of art and the one richest in variations; it has therefore been equally favoured by Indian painters and sculptors. The postures taken up by these couples do not always have an excessively erotic meaning since quite often the figures stand quietly next to each other, but it is striking that the majority of the groups of lovers are to be found on sacred buildings, even at the time of the earliest Buddhist art.

There are, for example, on the wall of the main entrance to the temple-hall at Kārla, several such groups, which have been interpreted by some experts as groups of donors but by the majority as representations of mithuna, as couples of lovers. Eventually both interpretations arrive at the same conclusion, since even such purely secular groups as those of donors point to the union of man and wife because of the strikingly sensual presentation of the individual figures. This tendency towards thinking in pairs which led to the frequent representation of couples of lovers was time and again confirmed by the shakti-dogma of later Indian religions, which adds to the male gods the corresponding female figures, since the might and power of the deities is seen as a unity composed of male and female elements. Here, too, the conception of the ancient mother-goddess forms the background, as the woman alone was thought able to personify both female and male qualities, beauty and strength, birth and death, life and destruction.

One superficial means of distinguishing between pairs of gods and pairs of human beings is the difference in size of man and woman in the former. In all truly religious works and all symbolic works the male god is the chief figure and is physically vastly superior. But this does not apply to the groups of donors or mithuna couples of early Buddhist art, nor to the images on the outer walls of mediaeval Hindu temples, where the size of the sexes is retained in the natural proportions.

In literature a distinction is made between married couples (dampati) and pairs of lovers (mithuna), but this is done only in a literary way and is not exactly confirmed anywhere. One of the reasons to designate the couples of Kārla and Kanheri as couples of donors was that the flowers in the hands of some of the figures were interpreted as offerings to the sanctuary, forming part of pūja, the religious rites. Strangely enough most of these couples turn their backs on the chaitya itself, and their images are not fixed inside the hall but on the walls of the entrance hall. Yet the flowers need not necessarily be thought of as sacrifices, but can also be explained as erotic symbols. What, however, is decisive is the fact that similar couples in Bodh Gayā and still more often in Nāgārjunakonda act in so erotic a way that there is hardly any doubt they must be interpreted as mithuna groups.

The images of these couples are frequently made of baked clay. Such terra-cotta plaques of the Shunga and Kushāna epochs from Rupar, Ahichhatra, and other sources are not only proof of the popularity of the theme but also of its more general meaning of its content which is bound neither to any particular religion and its cult nor to any special buildings (9). Generally speaking it is a kind of symbolism of fertility and thereby of good luck to ward off misfortune and as such had a right to a place in religious buildings. The loving and detailed reproduction of the subject is to be attributed to the general art of the Indian sculptors and painters, to the taste of the people and to the far-reaching tolerance of those who commissioned the images and of the monks living in the sanctuaries.

It is well known that the strict tenets of Buddhism with regard to salvation through one's own effort (the Enlightenment) reject sweet sensualism in all its forms as representing a tie with life, as an ever-repeated concatenation with one's existence on earth. Particularly dangerous for the man striving for and seeking salvation are women and female charms; the legend reports that shortly before his enlightenment even Buddha himself was surrounded and spied upon by the daughters of Māra, who tried to tempt him and deflect him from his goal. The images on Buddhist buildings, but also the yakshinīs and vrikshakās of Bhārhut and Sānchī mentioned earlier, seem to be less concerned with the threat to the moral tenets of Buddhism than with the devilish temptations by the daughters of Māra. One does not know precisely how accustomed the people of India were to this kind of nakedness at that time, but whatever their experience may have been one might maintain that prominent images like these must not have counteracted the ascetic leanings.

Coomaraswamy once said that early Buddhist art was an art specifying Buddhism, but not Buddhist art, and

this applies *cum grano salis* to all sacred Indian art. The old popular faith retained with regard to sex that earthy freshness which later all superior Indian religions had to acknowledge and to tolerate whether or not they wished to do so. Moreover, some comfort may have been derived from the thought that the images portrayed here were not to be worshipped but only to be contemplated, and, as it were, read. The observer or reader only passed by these gates, railings and vestibules on his way to the inner sanctuary, and the vrikshakās and yakshinīs and the mithuna-couples turned their backs on him; he, so to say, left them behind as they in their turn were to leave him behind when he stood before the stūpa, walked around it, and thus worshipped the Buddha.

The Buddhists, moreover, acted in a similar way in literature when they changed the outspoken popular stories and fairy-tales into jātakas, that is, reports of Buddha's rebirth, only adding a short moral lesson. In any case this so easily excused moral toleration has proved a true blessing to the lover of art, as Indian art could not have risen to its great height without the outstanding works of ancient Buddhist imagery; in a like manner the preservation of the old popular stories in the jātakas has proved a first-rate achievement of Indian civilization.

Going on from there straight to the art shown on the temple walls at Bhuvaneshvara, Konarak, and Khajurāho is a long step not alone in time but also with regard to the extreme intensification of the theme of eroticism. Indian erotic literature with its tendency to systematization already proves to be very influential here. As the Indian teachers of speech were the first to create a systematic grammar, so the erotics—Vātsyāyana gives in his *Kāmasūtra* a long list of names of his predecessors—created a grammar of the language of love, or rather of the practice of love, which was to be transposed into imageries on temple walls.

Simultaneously mention must be made of the orgiastic tantric cults, which, as we now know for certain, took place in the neighbourhood of these temples. A Sanskrit text on the architecture of temples, the *Shilpa Prakāsha*, written in the tantric period of Orissa between the ninth and the twelfth centuries A.D., reads: "Listen to the description of kāmabandha (the love imagery) ... desire is the root of the universe. All beings have been born through desire. The original matter and all beings are reabsorbed by desire. Without Shiva and Shakti creation could exist only in imagination. There would be neither birth nor death without the deeds of Kāma ... The science of kāmakalā (love-imagery) constitutes a large part of the *Āgamas*. Any place devoid of love-imagery is known as a 'place to be avoided'. According to Kaulācāra this is a lowly and forsaken place, an abyss as it were, which one avoids like the abode of death." (10) The continuity of matriarchal concepts can plainly be demonstrated in the tantric cults and proved by quotations from many a text.

With the original mithuna groups these mediaeval images share only the starting point and the fact that both of them are to be found on the outer walls of sanctuaries. But another study would have to deal in detail with the scenes and themes depicted there because of the independent and very special character of their eroticism.

The secularization of the love images is evident especially in miniature paintings, which also refer to the erotic literature as source. There the greatest variety of detail is to be found, the most subtle descriptions of the particular moods pertaining to the different ways and emotions of love. The *Kāmasūtra* and the *Rasikapriyā*, these copious works of literature describing the art of love, help in explaining these series of images which in fact are frequently to be found as illustrations of these works. A striking similarity of mood and visual melodies is shown also by the Bengal love-mysticism based upon the mediaeval worship of Vishnu.

In miniatures as in the following poem by Vidyāpati Thākur the nāyikā, the main figure, is often shown without a male partner yet her attitude and mood always refer to her lover. Strangely enough, crude pictures of the enjoyment of love are rare in this so definitely secular art, though they are to be found here and there. The art peculiar to miniatures uses the greatest refinement, frequently only giving slight hints. A knowledge of the language of images is essential to understand the individual types of women depicted in the miniatures, and one has to observe not only the garments, attitudes, and gestures of the woman as the chief figure but the secondary figures as well, and even the plants and objects disposed in a symbolic manner around her.

The above-mentioned poem by Vidyāpati Thākur might be illustrated by scores of Rājasthān and Pahari miniatures:

"Sakhi: The love of beautiful Rādhā is young,
No obstacle could restrain her;
She went alone,

Never did she mind the long way or any hardship.
She throws away her necklace, precious though it is,
Because it lies too heavy on her breasts;
She takes off her rings and her bracelets
And lets them lie there in the dust.

Jewels jingle around her feet:
She flings them off and hurries on;
The night is overcast and so black,
But love lights up the darkness.

Her path is surrounded by danger,
But the arms of love will conquer;
Vidyāpati calls out to her: This is true,
There never has been a creature like you" (11).

THE ACTIVE WOMAN

The imagery of this group is further removed from the background of the Indian past, which mainly depicted fertility and sex. The door is now thrown open to truly secular art, though this does not apply without exceptions. As the theme of motherhood is related to family life, so that of work forms part of the problems of the caste system, and it may be that artists were therefore somewhat chary of using it as a subject in their work. In any case there is hardly any civilization with an imagery which tells so little about the various activities of the people. Here and there one does come upon scenes of agricultural or domestic work where strict subjection to the caste system was evidently not thought to be compromising. More recent and present day imagery of India has freed itself from traditional restraints in an almost revolutionary way, but this is no doubt the influence of Western thought and art.

An exception is found only in the ancient Buddhist reliefs for which the problems of the caste system were less important; this applies mainly to the illustrations of the jātakas and to later miniatures; the latter depict, although from the point of view of the Mogul court and the Rājput principalities, life at court and rural life in great detail.

It is not easy to avoid generalizing and to state that there was in India only the contrast between housewife and mother on the one hand and the prostitute and partner in every kind of pleasure on the other, as literature and art seem to suggest. There was certainly also the hard working woman in the towns as well as in the villages, who was occupied in the trades or even in heavy physical work, as for example in public building. But there are only hidden hints of this, as when women in Mogul miniatures by chance appear carrying heavy weights in flat baskets on their heads; the same is to be seen in India today.

On the other hand the woman working in the kitchen is a frequent motif of miniature painting, and the busy cook is pronounced a saint as early as in the *Mahābhārata*; neglect of the household is severely denounced: "Where crockery or broken utensils or furniture are left lying about, where the house is sordid and brought to ruin by sinful living, there the women will perish." (12)

Stories from the youth of Krishna offered the Indian artist a chance of depicting the life of the gopis, the young shepherdesses among whom Krishna grew up; he fell in love with Rādhā, the most lovely of them. At first sight one hardly notices anything but the beauty of the village girl who gracefully balances the heavy pail of milk on her proudly held head; although this depicts a great physical effort, the observer does not think of the weight of the burden but only of such characteristics as the young woman's charm and gracefulness. It is the same with the numerous representations of servants; there, too, the young women are conceived as accessories to the scenes in the palaces, contrasting or harmonizing in their attitudes, bodily shapes and garments with the chief persons rather than appearing merely as working beings. Great importance is vouchsafed here as every-where to showing their physical charms and the symbolic harmony between them and the general idea of the image.

It is therefore not by chance that one meets images of "active" women like these again and again in the imagery of the rāgamālās wherever descriptions of emotional melodies are given; frequently stories are included of events from Krishna's life. There is for example the prince who meets at the well with the village girls as they draw water and then offer it to the thirsty traveller. Here the emotional content of the symbolism is evident: to quench the man's thirst stands for the promise of complying with the demands of his

Family of Shepherds with Animals   24

love. This melody has a name of its own: "Kumāh Rāga", that is "pot or jug melody". Usually there is in these rāgamālās a servant as partner of the heroine. She comforts her when she is deserted, accompanies her in her adventures, overhears her speaking of love, hands her the toilet utensils when she prepares for the expected visit of her lover—all emotions and images which are continually repeated in Indian erotic literature and its illustrations.

The servant's activities proper are restricted to a small number of functions: she presents vessels containing either drinks or food or cosmetics; she carries the fan and the sunshade—in the miniatures a cloth is sometimes shown instead of a fan; she helps her mistress with her bath and her more intimate toilet; or she attends to her while she smokes the hookah, the waterpipe, which women also were accustomed to smoke. There are a few other such duties in the care of the mistress, and the servants sometimes even carry arms to protect her. Although the majority of these representations are to be found in the later miniatures from the Mogul and Rājput courts, there are nevertheless comparable scenes to be found in the reliefs and paintings of ancient Indian art, particularly in the Gandhāra and

Yakshinī carrying a Vessel

Āndhra art. Thus there appear in the former for example armed women as Amazons at court. Similar figures are also to be found in the paintings of Ajantā. Not all the armed women are servants; in addition there are numerous armed goddesses, and princesses and ladies at court quite often take up arms, whether for hunting or for war.

Carrying is always regarded as a lowly activity; the wife carries the burdens for the husband, the servant for the mistress. Even for religious service, on the way to the temple when food or flowers are to be sacrificed by the mistress, the servant carries the basket with the gifts while the lady at best holds a single flower in her hand. This scene in particular is well known as the image of the melody which in the rāgamālās is called a "rāginī bhairavī", therefore a female melody and which usually shows the woman worshipping the symbol of the union of lingam and yoni.

One of the most frequent activities of women is gardening; the calling of mālinī, gardener or flower woman, was exclusively a female profession. She looked after an indispensable part of the decoration of the house and the women's adornment, because no beautiful woman should lack flowers in her hair and garlands around her neck. Hanging flower garlands forms to this day an essential item of Indian ceremonies, not only with regard to women. At farewell and at greeting assemblies, at weddings and at festivities, whenever honours or distinctions are conferred, flower garlands are presented as a sign of great respect and sincere sympathy. In the more ancient stories and fairy-tales the flower woman is often the confident and messenger of the heroine, frequently acting as her wet nurse and ayah, who herself is described as a good storyteller, in particular of fairy-tales. Yet she can assume the role of treacherous schemer and procuress just as easily as that of wise adviser.

Women worshipping
the Footprints left by Buddha

THE WOMAN DISPLAYING HER CHARMS

In this group and the next, certain other activities of women are treated together; they have no special professional character but are of a more general kind, such as the care of the woman's body and of her garments, as well as objects concerned with games and entertainments. Indian artists have made use of these activities principally to present woman in all her bodily charm and typically female moods, or—as one might say—to take her out of the seclusion of Indian every-day life and to let her be seen in intimate imagery by the enthusiast or lover.

Heinrich Zimmer maintains that an intimate knowledge of the female body cannot be gained from the observation of models or the memory of visual impressions alone. It is the product and the expression of the sense of touch, of a wide experience won in the intimacy of love; from this a happy intuition may derive the secret of inner life which reveals itself in the beauty of the female form (13). Here again a statement is deduced from analysis of the imagery which seems to contradict the moral tradition as it has been known from the ancient codes of law and been acknowledged by society. Who will believe that all the images of women in Indian art are based on imagination alone and intended to generalize and idealize a merely surmised reality?

Bathing women were repeatedly represented in the Kushāna art of Mathurā and later in the Ajantā paintings of the Gupta and post-Gupta periods; this then became one of the favourite themes of miniature painting. The images of single women as well as of groups of bathing women, as they often appear for example in the story of Krishna, who had stolen the garments of the gopīs, gave the artists the means of showing naked or partly naked female bodies with all their charms. The artists were, however, rarely eager to depict complete nakedness, and enhanced its sensual effect by adding ornamental chains, wraps, partially concealing veils, and by showing the anxious endeavours of the women to cover with their hands whatever nudity was still apparent. The water surface too, though shown as transparent, usually lets the observer see only floating outlines. One therefore finds here the opposite of the representation of ancient types of women based on the concept of the mother-goddess: there the genitals of the women were shown bare as signs of female fertility; this can still be observed in extant examples of ancient Indian art. There can, however, be no doubt about the erotic intention of miniature painting, notwithstanding the endeavours to use conceiling veils; this is only the outcome of the refinement which eroticism underwent as civilization progressed.

A special form of this group is the woman at home in the act of dressing, a frequent theme in miniatures called "Rādhā adorns herself for the visit of Krishna". This usually affords the artist the opportunity of letting the maiden's hair hang down in damp and long strands, while it is usually set with care; quite often there is somewhere hidden at the edge of the picture a man, Krishna, to be seen watching her. It may be noted that the motif of the heroine drying her hair in the sun is often to be found in the popular fairy-tales of India, particularly in Bengal. Usually the maiden on the roof of the house is discovered, with her hair undone, by a suitor passing by on horseback, who then falls in love with her. Most of the women are shown in the miniatures either standing or squatting on low stools; jugs, cans, cups and small receptacles for ointment are disposed around her conveniently to hand. Some of the passages in classical Indian literature mention explicitly that the breasts and the armpits have to be bared while the hair is being combed (14).

In the process of dressing the women use thin paint-brushes for their eyes; the soot from lamps (ānjana) is used to blacken the edge of the lids, and an ointment for the eyes is mentioned which was supposed to help in the finding of hidden treasures (15). Other tints too are employed as means for beautification. Coloured and scented oils were rubbed into the body and auspicious patterns were painted on the soles of the feet and the palms of the hands with red lacquer-colour (16).

The woman with the mirror constitutes another of the themes showing the progress of dressing. One side of the round bronze mirror, which the woman usually holds by a short handle, is always highly polished so as to give a clear reflection. Mirrors like these are known from excavations conducted in the towns of the Harappa period. The decorative panels in the railings of the stūpa at Bhārhut, dating from early Buddhist times, show women holding such mirrors. These were then retained as popular attributes of female deities, especially of the goddess Pārvatī, the wife of Shiva. But the yakshinīs too and later the devasundarīs carry mirrors; since the Middle Ages these mirrors have been more distinctly curved, and their handles, shaped like knobs, were fixed

at their backs. Mirror-scenes were also a subject of miniatures, but there most of the mirrors are framed, are larger and square and are held by a servant. A rāginī, the bilāval (or bilāvar) rāginī is typical of this kind of image, which affords the artist an opportunity of showing the beautiful features of the woman in two profile views facing each other.

One attitude shown repeatedly on the walls of mediaeval Indian temples as well as in some miniatures is that of the thorn-extractor, a theme well known from classical European art, although there it is associated with the figure of a young boy (the *spinario*). In Khajurāho the body of a woman trying to extract a thorn is twisted into an extravagent position, the injured foot turned by 180 degrees toward her body, and then turned upward. It should be noted that the attitudes of the thorn-extractor and that of the woman painting the soles of her feet are presented in a very similar way and can therefore be easily mistaken one for the other. In the miniatures it is sometimes a servant's duty to extract the thorn which her impetuous mistress has run into her foot as she hastened to meet her lover. An image of two women by a Bengal woodcarver leaves the observer guessing whether they are occupied extracting a thorn or painting the soles of their feet.

Here mention should be made of the letter-writing girl; like the thorn-extractor and the mirror-holding devasundarī, she formed a frequent ornament of the walls of mediaeval temples. In the Rietberg Museum at Zurich there is a sculpture of a woman holding a small letter in her hand; this figure was noticed by Mrs Lohuizen de Leeuw and compared with the imagery of the Keshava temple in Belur and the sculpture of the Khajurāho temple mentioned above (17). This may well be a nāyikā writing to her absent lover, since according to Mrs de Leeuw there might have been quite a close connection between the surasundarī images and the rāgamālā cycle.

It is only a small step from the care of the body to the things especially enjoyed by women, games and arts. The scanty consideration with which work requiring physical exertion was treated in Indian art and literature led in striking contrast to an over-valuation of the leisure activities of women, probably idealizing the actual situation on purpose. Of course this applies mainly to the entertainments of women of the privileged classes, in particular to those at the courts of greater or lesser prin-

Woman holding a Mirror

ces, an exception being made only by some rural pastimes and festivities, for example the holi-feast in the miniatures illustrating the series of the Krishna stories.

Much favoured, although not too often represented, was the young maidens' game of ball. The *Mahābhārata* mentions (18) it as do also the stories from the aristocratic circles contained in the *Dashakumāracarita* (19). Special stress is laid in these stories on the bright colours of the balls. In the *Bhāgavata-Purāna* there is a story about Shiva visiting Vishnu, when the latter created by magic an enchantingly beautiful maiden. While she played with a ball the wind carried off her garments. Shiva hastened to follow the temptress (20). A relief from Mathurā, unfortunately badly damaged, shows a maiden balancing a ball on her raised elbow.

Another open-air pastime was the use of swings. Again there are in the rāgamālā whole groups of illustrations of this charming activity; usually playmates and servants took part in the game by setting the swing in motion (rāga hindola). This swing had a broad seat on which the lovers, usually Krishna and Rādhā, could comfortably find place. There are, however, less conventional pictures too with a much smaller swing hanging from a tree, where the maidens with their hair flying in the wind enjoy their happy game. The most famous representation of this kind is a mural painting in cave III of Ajantā, which shows a princess on a swing as illustration to a jātaka.

To indoor entertainments belong the various games using boards, especially chess which is of Indian origin. There, however, the display of the female body is of less importance than that of the woman's pensive mood, probably indicating either future love or an unhappy love experience in the past. The women at the princely courts also indulged in the vice of smoking and are therefore frequently represented sucking at the long tube of the Indian waterpipe, the hookah, sometimes surrounded by servants or lonely and thoughtful. The drunk woman, quite often depicted in early Buddhist times, seems to have belonged not to the class of noble women but to that of the prostitutes and courtesans living in towns. If the stories and fairy-tales are to be believed, these were held in high esteem and, like the hetaerae in ancient Greece, were thought worthy to be the companions of illustrious men. In the life of Buddha himself there were such women acting as charitable benefactresses. Sometimes, however, drinking couples are represented, since according to Indian erotics, stimulating drinks greatly increase the enjoyment of love.

There is further a considerable number of representations of this group showing larger or smaller social gatherings of women, of which the most lovely instances belong to the Āndhra art of Amarāvatī and Nāgārjunakonda and to the murals of Ajantā. In creating these images the artists are intent at times on contrasting the poise of the mistress with the lively gestures of her playmates and servants, and at times on showing the variety of movements in groups of women in early Buddhist art, worshipping the empty throne of Buddha or depicted asleep in palace-scenes. The chief endeavours of other artists are concentrated on showing the rhythmic homogeneity of attitudes, for example in a wonderful group of praying women in a cave of the rock at Aurangabad. A simplification, a synopsis as it were, of these compositions, is provided by the numerous groups of two figures, usually pairs of friends or of mistress and servant, many of which are to be found among the famous ivory plaques of Begram and much later in the miniatures from various Indian schools. Here too the variety of gradations, the contrasts and the rhythm of the composition are decisive for the display of female charms.

Finally, two large sub-sections of this group which were of great importance in the development of Indian art must be examined, namely the dancing woman and the woman-musician. The characteristics mentioned above are to be found here too, adapted of course to the requirements of the traditionally regulated dance-movements and to the use of the classical Indian musical instruments. The dance is one of the highest forms in the representation of divine power attained in Indian art, and is to be seen in particular in the images of the cosmic dance of Shiva. Generally speaking the postures peculiar to dancing have influenced mainly the representation of single figures, where the positions are shown in a contrapuntal balance, dancing as it were even when at rest. Group-dances belong even today almost exclusively to the folk-dances and to the tribal dances.

The majority of the classic Indian dances are performed today by women who take also the parts of men, for example that of the god Shiva, and this seems to have applied in earlier times too. To mention only a few of the better known instances: the apsarās and the gandharvas dance in Indra's heaven and the divine king refuses to miss any of these entertainments and is very angry when

31

a human being tries to abduct one of these celestial dancers. A lovely group of female dancers and musicians is represented in a relief on a stone pillar of the enclosure (railings) of the stūpa at Bhārhut; it is a very clear illustration of the contrasting movements of the dancers who are standing or sitting, and of the sitting musicians who accompany the dance with their instruments and with rhythmic clapping. A more individualistic dance is represented by a relief from Pawaya, dating from the Gupta period. Here too the dance is confined to women, but more instruments seem to be used. There are a great variety of dance compositions, a consequence of the Indian tendency to make systematic divisions. It is an open secret that the revival and renewal of the classic Indian dance in recent decades was based chiefly on the earlier imagery with its minute details to be seen for example on the walls of the temples of Chidambaram. Compared with these stone sculptures the miniature paintings are of less significance, as they show dances created partly under Mogul influence at the princely courts which therefore differ from the traditional forms of the old Indian dances. Some miniatures,

however, contained in early Jain manuscripts, form an exception to the rule. One very popular motif deserves special mention here: Rādhā dancing in the presence of Krishna, her lover.

Quite often music and dance are performed by one and the same person; in folk-dancing in particular the dancer accompanies himself on a rhythmic instrument. It seems to have been one of the main duties of female servants to add with music and dance to the entertainment of the ruling couple or the court. The goddess Sarasvatī is characterized by a musical instrument called the vīnā. Women musicians are a favourite theme of the rāgamālas; in the rāginī vasanta, the spring melody, Krishna dances in a circle formed by the shepherdesses who accompany him on their instruments. The todi rāginī, and in a similar way the rāginī dakshina gurjarī, shows a lonely vīnā player among the beasts of the wood. Even a remotely complete description of Indian music and dance scenes would exceed the frame set for this study of the characterization of the various groups, and it must therefore suffice to point out here once more the great popularity of these themes in Indian art as a whole.

Women Dancers

THE FEMALE CHARACTER AND FEMALE MOODS

The physical charm of woman is less stressed in this grouping than in the previous one; rather it is her inmost character and moods that are the artist's concern. To it belong the greater part of the melodies assembled in the rāgamālās, the images of the nāyikās according to the texts of the *Rasikapriyā*, the *Amarushataka*, and other similar poems. Two other important groups of motifs have, however, been included, which in part are similar to the illustrations of the rāgamālās but which at the same time represent a considerably older tradition, and probably some deeper symbolism: the woman amidst plants, especially trees, or with animals, the peacock or the parrot in particular; and the woman at the window or at the door looking around, full of curiosity, a motif of deeper meaning than would at first appear.

There are various traditions concerning miniatures inspired by music, the rāgas and rāginīs, male and female melodies, to which belongs the third group of "sons" as rāgas. These chief, secondary, and subsidiary melodies, grouped in families, form the extensive system of the rāgamālās, "melody garlands", all of which show distinctive marks regarding their musical as well as their iconographic character (21). The names of these representations of sentiments and emotions, adapted each to a certain melody, refer to Indian landscapes or deities, to special natural phenomena, to the seasons, months, and so on. The translation of rāga as "melody" does not correspond exactly to the Indian word. According to Gangoly a rāga ought to be defined as a "composition of musical notes (svaras), having a sequence, form or structure of a peculiar significance. Some of its component notes stand in a significant relationship to one another so that they give a special character to each rāga." (22) Rāgas and emotions (shringāra) are equivalent. Animals and plants assume a symbolic character in these imageries.

The nāyakas and nāyikās (heroes and heroines), who are partly identical with the figures of the rāgamālās, belong to a similar system of sentiments of which a great variety of contrasts is to be noted. The principal contrasts are formed by unfortunate love and separation (virāha) as opposed to fortunate love and reunion (samyoga). There are numerous subdivisions of the nāyikās; a major role is played by the three groups of the bashful (mugdhā), of the partly bashful, partly bold (madhyā) and of the bold women (praudhā). Inside these groups the clearly outlined love relations of women are defined as forming different types described in their minutest details. For instance: "Wise men call a woman an abhishārikā nāyikā who is made restless by her love, is devoid of bashfulness, and who having adorned herself steals at night to someone else's house seeking there the enjoyment of love." A total of about three hundred and sixty types of this kind are enumerated. The *Rasikapriyā* by Kesavadās Mishra (approximately 1555 to 1617), a theoretical study published in honour of Krishna, treats the emotions of lovers in a similar way.

There is a great variety in Indian art in the different kinds of links existing between women and trees. Simple narrative scenes are frequent where a woman is seen standing in front of a tree or beside it, climbing up or sitting in its branches, touching the trunk with her foot or reaching upward into the boughs. But there are also scenes with a symbolic composition where the image increases and completes the meaning of the theme: these include trees symmetrically flanking the scene, or the overlapping of tree trunks and female bodies so that the top of the tree shows above the woman's head as if it were to crown the woman's body. Furthermore there are representations where the branches seem to grow directly out of the shoulders and sides of the woman. All this goes to show, as mentioned in the introduction and in the paragraphs about goddesses, that a close inner connection was assumed to exist between the growth of plants and feminine nature, based on the original conceptions of a fertility goddess personifying human as well as plant life.

The similarity between female nature and that of plants is, however, not supposed to be restricted to growth and fertility—which were symbolized according to ancient Indian concepts by the kalpavriksha tree. It was thought to be founded also on visual similarities; to describe this always gave great pleasure to Indian poets and artists. Thus the thin trunk was compared to the slim limbs of the woman; the winding branches and twigs, the creepers, and the air-roots hanging down were thought to resemble the gestures and movements of the woman. Comparisons have also frequently been made with the beauty of blossoms, and some fruits have been likened to the swelling or still tender round forms of the young female body. Studying the imageries one has therefore always to consider this train of thought of the Indian artists and to remember that to depict reality, as for example in a landscape, was of less importance than to probe deeper into the mutual character of women and plants by examining the similarities and dissimilarities of the superficial likeness of form, and thus to characterize the women's emotions.

There is a wonderfully poetic description of the creation of woman which points to her connection with other natural phenomena, though not only as far as plants are concerned. When Tvashtri, the divine creator, wanted to create woman, he found that he had used up all his material in creating man and that not a single piece of solid matter was left over. He thought it over carefully and then took the sphere of the moon, the windings of creepers, the pliancy of the tendrils, the trembling of the grasses, the towering thinness of the reeds, the freshness of the blossoms, the weightlessness of the leaves, the reduced outline of the elephant's trunk, the glance of the deer's eyes, the loose order of the bees' swarm, the happy shine of the sun's rays, the weeping lament of the clouds, the unreliability of the wind, the shyness of the hare, the vanity of the peacock, the softness of the parrot's chest, the extraordinary hardness of the diamond, the sweetness of honey, the cruelty of the tiger, the warm glow of embers, the coldness of snow, the loquacity of the jay, the enticing call of the cuckoo, the hypocrisy of the crane, the loyalty of the partridge—all this the god mixed together, created woman, and gave her to man (23).

A text like this explains better than other words could do the pictures that belong to this book, and, if there were still any doubt, it would be easy to find also a connection between female nature and other natural phenomena, by making similar comparisons. Of course there are also in the groupings mentioned earlier objects connected with the images of women, which are likened in a similar manner to the form of the female body. For instance jugs of water (or milk) and vessels filled with plants are believed to be auspicious and are set up at festivities, and because of their convex shape, are likened to the high breasts of beautiful women (24).

While women and trees had always been found together on many an image in Bhārhut, Sānchī and Mathurā, this combination no doubt formed the core of the vast majority of the images of the rāgamālās and of most of the nāyikās. The utkā nāyikā waits for her lover, supporting herself on a tree under which she has already prepared a bed of leaves. The vipralabdhā nāyikā, too, went to a meeting at night, but then was left alone for a long time

34

because her lover failed to come. Lamenting, she turned to the tender little tree; its leaves were torn off and lay on the ground. Sorrowful and nervous she had plucked off almost all of them, nearly stripping the small plant. The abhishārikā hurries through the benighted wood, past dark and threatening trees with all kinds of serpents and creeping worms emerging from behind them. Even the ganikā or veshyā, the courtesan from the town, likes to stay in her garden so rich in trees and flowers, resting her full and heavy figure on the long-leaved banana plants.

An ancient motif in Indian literature and art is the dohada or ashokadohada, which consists in touching the ashoka tree with the foot to make it flower (25). In the *Agnipurāna* (26) there is a passage where women and young girls holding each others' hands dance around a tree, then clasp it in their arms with the kanthasutra embrace and sacrifice saffron paste to it. The touching of trees by a single person has been used as a theme for images in the art of Bhārhut and is still used, while the round dance around a tree has continued to be used as illustration of the Krishna legend even till recent times.

As did the outstanding Indian art historian Sivarama-murti one may perhaps add to the type of images on which trees and maidens are shown together the so-called stambhaputtalikā, those of maiden beside a pillar. The pillars of the enclosure railings at Bhārhut and the very numerous imageries of Kushāna art at Mathurā are proof of the popularity of this motif, which belongs to the same groups of motifs as the dohada and vrikshakā images already noted. Sivaramamurti quotes passages from the *Raghuvamsha* and the *Rāmāyana* (27). In many of the large number of wonderful representations of women in Indian miniatures Rādhā, the shepherdess whom Krishna loved, is shown in profile, carrying in her hands blossoms symbolizing her thoughtful mood and her longing for her lover. This flower is usually related to the physical appearance of the maiden: a round flower on a short stem is carried by a dainty round-faced Kāngrā girl, while the slim young lady with the long limbs of a Kishangar miniature holds long-stemmed gently swaying blossoms in her hand.

Side by side with the representation of trees, scenes with animals of an unmistakably symbolic character should also be mentioned. The peacock with its shining plumage and its little crown of feathers plays an outstanding role in this erotic symbolism. He always appears when the kakubha rāginī is shown and probably indicates the mood of a dull and rainy day which naturally corresponds to the melancholy adventures of the loving woman. Falcons on the wrist of a noble lady do not point directly to resignation, although the fast flight of the bird is to be interpreted as symbolizing the lady's longing in pursuit of her absent lover. There are frequent images of the cakora, a kind of partridge, supposed to feed on the rays of the moon and thereby symbolizing night and longing desires. But it is the various kinds of parrots which are represented most often; conversations with the speaking bird play an important part in Indian stories and popular fairy-tales. These birds are taken for playmates by the maidens or women and further assume the functions of an adviser or of a spy appointed by the absent husband. Small monkeys may be used as simple playthings and also cats, the latter often arousing the anger of the woman when they tease the bird and have to be pursued with the mistress's stick. In scenes where maidens are shown waiting or hurrying outside, birds and other animals living in the woods, particularly antelopes and deer, are often depicted in addition to the birds kept in the garden and to other domestic animals.

This art of animal symbolism was fully developed in miniature paintings but foreshadowed in many works of art of more ancient epochs. In the sculptures at Mathurā for instance the women often hold a bird or a bird cage in their hands, symbols which here probably indicate a readiness for love; this agrees well with the meaning of the small groups of erotic figures at the top of the pillars. Lately, Mrs Lohuizen de Leeuw has pointed out that in the mediaeval sculptures small animals, such as scorpions and lizards, gave the women a chance to open and lift up their garments in order to discover the mischief-maker crawling along their bodies. Of course among the symbolic animals must be counted those mentioned above, which were originally related to certain deities and served as their vāhana or vehicle. As smaller figures they frequently filled empty spaces and indicated characteristics of secular and erotic emotions. The supposition cannot be ruled out that they were included as reminders of animal-husbands, frequently the heroes of popular fairy-tales (28).

A special meaning is attached to another subject in this group: that of a woman at the window or at the door. Superficially observed this is a simple, worldly motif which shows the woman as an inquisitive spectator, usually at the side of some larger scene. In this sense it is known in Sanskrit literature, where beautiful women standing at the windows are mentioned when towns are described; a passage of the *Raghuvamsha* reads: "In the daytime the lovely features of the maidens and at night the brilliance of the lamps light up the windows of the houses." (29)

Yet the connection of a woman with a door, gate or entrance, or that of a woman at a window, seems to have a deeper symbolic meaning. Here the display of the woman has been made the main theme, but her association with an opening has a meaning similar to that of representations of the goddess of fertility or the mother-goddess, dealt with in the earlier part of this study. In the small sculptures of early times one often meets with a kind of exhibitionism, where the characteristics of sex are stressed, being regarded as an indication of fertility. Though scenes in which women show themselves at windows or doors in town houses can hardly anymore be interpreted as a ritual divestment pointing to fertility, it is nevertheless possible that the idea had persisted as an auspicious symbolism and as a remembrance of more ancient concepts. In a few imageries, notably some small reliefs above the lintels of the doors of temples in Bhu-vaneshvara, women are shown squatting in the so-called delivery-chair; they reveal the survival of a sex-symbol-ism, just as the Indian popular art has always retained it, and even the developed Shivaite religion makes plentiful use of the symbols of lingam and yoni, phallus and vulva. More recent conceptions display a more outspoken eroticism, seeking to attract in a cruder manner and also laying greater stress upon the more general female charms.

Images of this kind are very frequent in early Buddhist art, where the woman at the so-called chaitya window may figure as an individual motif; she is, however, sometimes included in scenes, as for instance in the famous medallion-relief of Amarāvatī where she watches Buddha taming an elephant which has run wild. The ivory reliefs at Begrām, mentioned above, repeatedly show maidens in pleasing postures filling up the inside of a gateway of the Sānchī-toranas type. In the Kushāna art of Mathurā, from the Ajantā paintings to the miniatures, the same theme is to be found, but with an increasingly secular meaning. It is not unusual to see in the illustrations of the Krishna legend the maidens who accompany Rādhā standing in front of the door or hiding behind it or looking out of the windows of the neighbouring houses. Popular art on the other hand, for instance the reliefs on the terra-cotta temples of Bengal, continued to use this motif in recent times, but with stronger symbolic meaning and faithfully retaining the original content of the symbol in a way which is quite general in popular art.

Woman in Confinement on so-called Delivery-chair, assisted by Servants 36

PORTRAITS
OF WOMEN

Although portraits, especially those in painting, are fairly often referred to in literature, none has been preserved from ancient times which could with certainty be designated as such. The occasional representation of the heroines of history, or of religious legends or of epic literature, as, for example, of the mothers of Buddha and of Mahāvīra or of Sītā, the wife of Rāma, or of Krishna's beloved Rādhā, cannot be counted as true portraits, because there could have been no genuine models for them; the same applies to the mother and foster mother of Krishna.

All individual features are therefore missing and one can at best speak of ideal conceptions of these personalities, which lift them out of their surroundings and ascribe to them a certain attitude, certain garments and other details, and in this way build up a distinctive type of figure with fixed outlines.

Literature is rich in proofs of the existence of portraits, reaching back to the Gupta period. The classical dramatic art, as also the stories and fairy-tales, frequently describes how the love of the hero or heroine was awakened by an appearance in a dream, later confirmed by a real portrait of the beloved, which then led to the search for such a person (30). Naturally it is not known whether these portraits were true likenesses or based on idealized conceptions. Even the few remains of this kind that are available from later Indian art, for example the portraits of southern Indian rulers (31), show no signs of the reproduction of individual features, and this confirms the view shared by most scholars that India never knew the art of portraiture as it is understood in the West.

But this seems to be contradicted by the portraits in the miniatures, for among them there are representations of some Mogul rulers which are undoubtedly likenesses, even by the most exacting standards. Nevertheless the pictures of women constitute an exception even in this group, as it is uncertain whether it was at all permissible to paint their portraits from nature and to distribute them.

In principle therefore the general rules for the representation of women in Indian art hold good for the so-called portraits. The question of associating a system of idealized conceptions and a particular standard of values with a particular period or a particular region has been discussed above in connection with plants and animals. Even a modern artist like Abanindranath Tagore, the nephew of the famous poet, compares the legs of women to the trunks of banana trees growing down to the soil, their eyes to the delicate and fugitive fish, hastening to and fro like wagtails, moist and shimmering like lotus blossoms (32). Here movement alone seems significant, nothing is said about any single feature or characteristic trait, still less about any ugly details which might have helped to identify some particular figure. In these comparisons the face forms only part of the image and not the most essential one. Time and again the woman's figure is given prominence, as well as her attitude and gestures; the characteristics of sex too are usually given importance, the female breast is compared to a cloud (payas) as the donor of fluid, milk, or water (33).

THE CONCEPTION
OF FEMALE BEAUTY
IN INDIAN ART

What has been said up to now will have made it clear that the representation of women in Indian art cannot be judged from an aesthetic point of view which takes the individual personality of the female figure as starting point; all discussion has to be based on generally valid conceptions of beauty comprising as well as the body of the woman, her jewels and garments, her movements and gestures. It may therefore be expedient to quote—independent of the attached illustrations, yet running parallel to them—some of the descriptions of women well known from classical literature. Although these passages refer to certain personalities, to the Western mind they give no indication of any traits by which one could distinguish one woman from another.

The *Mahābhārata* for instance contains the following description of the heavenly nymph Urvashī: "Shining in her soft and curly long hair, which she had adorned with a great many jasmine blossoms, she strolled along and challenged, as it were, the moon itself by her moonlike face, so attractive through the movements of her brows, the sweet chatter of her mouth, its charm and gentle loveliness. Her breasts with their beautiful nipples, spread with an ointment of heavenly scented sandalwood, danced about as she walked, shining under her necklace. At every step the uprising and lively movement of her heavy breasts bent her down over her beautiful waist, girded by the three folds of her shining belt. Below it there shimmered, spread out like a mountain, raised and swelling like the slope of a hill, the temple of the god of love, surrounded by splendour, adorned by the ribbon of the belt, tempting and alarming the heart even of the celestial rishis: the faultless secret parts, veiled by a thin garment. The feet with the ankle joints embedded deep into them were hung with little bells. The long red toes and the feet shone like the vaulted back of a tortoise. Her appearance was further enhanced by her happy contentment, her loving mood and her coquetry as if she had partaken of some intoxicating drink." (34)

Draupadī, the heroine of the *Mahābhārata*, has black curls, eyes long like the leaf of the autumnal lotus, a scent like lotus in autumn, her face resembles the lotus blossom and, when covered with perspiration, that of the jasmine; her waist is slim, her hair long, her mouth red. She is neither too tall nor too short, her hips are lovely. She is not too thin nor too red, nor covered with too much hair. In yet another passage she is characterized by the following words: "Her ankle joints do not stick out and her thighs are firm and buxom. Three features are deep: voice, intelligence and navel; six are arched: her nose, eyes, ears, nails, breasts and the joints of her neck; five are red: the palms of her hands and feet, the corners of her eyes, her tongue, her nails; her speech is soft like that of the swan, her eyebrows and her eyes are round and arched, her lips are red like the bimba fruit, her neck is like a shell, her veins are hidden, her face resembles the full moon ... She is over-beautiful like a mare from Kashmir." (35)

Yet one more passage speaks of the same Draupadī, and it is interesting to observe the divergent and in part quite different description, but which is also given in general terms: "Could there be anyone in all the world who would not succumb to the power of love when he sees the magnificent moon of your face endowed with incomparable beauty, and sees the moonlight of the smile in your eyes and eyelashes, your lovely face covered by heavenly rays, delightful in its heavenly charm. Your magnificent breasts, those well-shaped breasts, fat and round breasts, touching one another and leaving no space between them, they resemble the buds of the lotus and—oh you with the lovely brows, you charming, smiling one—they incite me as with the branches of thorn of the god of love. When I see your waist, bent down by the weight of your breasts, when—oh you slim one—I see that waist which I can encircle with my fingers, then your secret parts, vaulted like the island in the river, assail me with incurable love-sickness. Oh you with the lovely hips, quench with the rain of your surrender and the cloud of joyful copulation the blazing fire of my love." (36)

There are seven more fine and tender characteristics of beauty designated by numbers: skin, hair, fingers, toes and the joints of the fingers and toes.

It is not easy to pick out from a general Indian theory of beauty a special study of that of women, as there is no critical literature dealing with this particular subject; any attempt at it has therefore to make use of the details from passages in Indian literature, like those quoted above, and from the general imagery. There exist, however, a great number of theoretical works on Indian art, in particular on architecture, painting, and sculpture. Sculpture and painting are very closely linked with the dance and music in India; it has been said for example: "Who ignores the rules of citra (painting, but also art in general) cannot understand the character of imagery. Without any knowledge of the dance, it is difficult to understand the rules of citra, and the dance again cannot be understood without some knowledge of music." And to quote another passage in the same work: "For citra as for the dance tradition requires the imitation of all the three worlds. The eyes and their expression, the limbs, arms and legs have to be used exactly in the same way as in the dance." (37)

The notion of citra in the Indian theory of art has a very wide range. Whatever there may be in the three worlds, mobile or immobile, if represented according to its own nature, is called citra; this notion is used in the *Shilparatna* and in the *Vishnudharmottara*. (38) From these passages one may conclude that not only earthly phenomena but also deities and their surroundings could be represented. All this had, however, to be confined in a frame of possibility and likelihood, so that an intelligent artist would limit his work and never attempt anything beyond possibility. While the genuine reproduction of actually visible phenomena was recommended in the depiction of what was earthly, in the representation of transcendental phenomena literary patterns were to be used. Though nobody would be likely to suggest the existence of naturalism in Indian art even less than that of individualism, it is noteworthy that the Indian theory of art uses notions of that kind, but in a very special sense. It must also be pointed out that, notwithstanding the scarcity of portraits, the theoretical works stress the value of a close relationship of the work of art to natural models, and recommend that recourse should be had at least to such authorities as give detailed descriptions of the imaginary. Portraiture and likeness to nature play a prominent part in the legends about the origin of the art of imagery.

As shown by literary sources the theory of the beauty of women in Indian art is chiefly concerned with the representation of female charms; it starts, however, from the anatomy of the female body and then goes on to the interpretation of the sexual attraction of women and their function with regard to fertility and motherhood. The effectiveness of the purely physical attributes is shown to be increased by attitudes, movements, and gestures, and jewelry and garments serve as a further attraction. But the main function of the attitudes and gestures is to show that variety of emotions and to indicate the ways in which they may be expressed with greater diversity. The representation of these emotions or moods and their expression is helped by reference to similar phenomena in animal and plant life, in fact in all nature, and also by the addition of various attributes. The whole system of representation is subjected to strict traditional rules.

There is, for example, the characteristic attitude of the woman, consisting of the threefold bend, the tribhanga-attitude, which displays particularly well the grace of the female body, though it can also be transferred to the man's body, where it appears (as mentioned before) as effeminate. Another typical movement which is often represented is the excessive protrusion—as it were vaulting—of the hips (atibhanga), used in particular by women carrying a child, but also by single figures without any special explanation through the significance of the image.

Innumerable are the gestures of the hands (mudrās), whereby the position of the fingers determines the meaning. The movement of the eyes is of great importance; somewhat less important is that of the legs and feet, which take up certain basic positions as they also do in dances. There is a great variety of jewelry which reaches from the hair, the face proper (that is the forehead, the ears, and nose), over all the body, and down to the ankles and toes. To how great an extent all women's clothing and make-up was subjected to strict regulations may be gauged from the sixteen basic rules governing the degree of attention to be given the dressing of any self-respecting woman, as passed on by Abu'l Fazl: "A bath, an oil massage, a careful setting of the hair, fixing a jewel and some paste of sandalwood to the forehead, a becoming dress, a caste-mark made with antimony to be added to the eyes, pendants for the earlobes, a pearl or ring of gold for the nose, a necklace or a garland, red henna for the palms of the hands, a belt around the hips, preferably decorated with small bells, jewelry for the feet, betel leaves for chewing, and finally well trained and dignified manners." (39)

Abanindranath Tagore, the Bengal artist, has drawn the attention of scholars to the theory of art (in six chapters) which is to be found in the commentary of Yasodhara to the *Kāmasūtra*. These six chapters (shad-anga) on art refer to the following essentials of art: one: rūpabheda, differentiation of form; two: pramānas, measures and proportions; three; bhāva-yojanā, the reproductions of emotions through which rasa is created; four: lāvanya-yojanā, the creation of beauty; five: sadrishya, similarity or the outcome of true observation; six: varnika-bhanga, differentiation of colours (40). These six basic rules, increased to eight by some other authors, seem to apply to all works of art, sculpture and painting, whether secular or sacred; they are of course not especially conceived so as to be applied to images of women, though at least two of the rules, those referring to emotions and beauty, do seem to be especially directed towards them.

The picture of the woman in Indian art, which is indicated here only in outline, is one that developed over a period of several thousands of years in figural art, literary parallels, and theoretical notions. In a study of this kind pre-eminence had naturally to be given to its special theme to set it up as clearly as possible; many other points of importance in the history of Indian art had therefore to be neglected, and it is only fair to state here that the author is conscious of this one-sidedness. For the lover and admirer of Indian civilization the representation of women in art will always be entitled to occupy a prominent place. This may help to set right some wrong conceptions of the position of women in the history of Indian civilization and to arrive at a correct judgment of the role played by them both past and present.

NOTES
AND BIBLIOGRAPHY

Notes and bibliography have been restricted to what seemed indispensable, but some works of more general purport, which may be of interest to the reader, are mentioned in the Notes or enumerated in the short list preceding them. Several of the books cited there contain illustrations which, because of the restricted space, could not be reproduced in the present study.

Altekar, A.S., The Position of Women in Hindu Civilization. Benares 1938, 2nd ed. 1956
Baktay, E., Die Kunst Indiens. Budapest/Berlin 1965
Franz, H.G., Buddhistische Kunst Indiens. Leipzig 1965
Franz, H.G., Hinduistische Kunst Indiens. Leipzig, to come out
Law, B.C., Women in Buddhist Literature. Ceylon 1927
Gunasinghe, Siri, "La Forme féminine dans la sculpture Pré-Gupta", in: Arts asiatiques, III, 2, Paris 1956
Rowlands, J.H., La Femme bengale dans la littérature du Moyen-Age. Paris 1930
Winternitz, M., "Die Frau in den indischen Religionen", in: Archiv für Frauenkunde und Eugenetik, vols. II/III, Leipzig 1920

1 Mention may here be made of the rediscovery of a book which the author, Niklas Müller (1770–1851), wrote in 1822 to defend Indian art against the attacks by upholders of the "classicist" theory of art. *Müller, N.*, Glauben, Wissen und Kunst der alten Hindus. Mainz 1822; facsimile reprint by Edition Leipzig 1968. In his essay in the Buddhist Yearly, vol. 1966, Heinz Kucharski indicated the importance of this book; he is preparing a new edition of the volume.

2 See *A.K.Coomaraswamy*, Geschichte der Indischen und Indonesischen Kunst. Leipzig 1927, for example p. 129. Also: *S.Kramrisch*, Grundzüge der indischen Kunst. Hellerau 1924; *S.Kramrisch*, "Die indische Kunst", in: *Springer*, Handbuch der Kunstgeschichte, vol. VI, Leipzig 1929

3 *Nehru, Jawaharlal*, Preface to: Women of India, ed. by Tara Ali Baig, p. VII, Delhi 1958

4 Concerning the role of women see: Bengalische Märchen, ed. by H.Mode and Arun Ray, Leipzig 1967

5 *Sivaramamurti, C.*, "Sanskrit Literature and Art-mirrors of Indian Culture", in: Memoirs of the Archaeological Survey of India, No. 73, Delhi 1955; this repeatedly draws the attention to secular art.

6 See the thorough new work by *Odette Viennot*, Les Divinités fluviales Gangā et Yamunā..., Paris 1964

7 See *Meyer, J.J.*, Das Weib im Altindischen Epos. Leipzig 1915, p.38

8 See chapter V, "Das Weib als Mutter", in the above-mentioned work by *J.J.Meyer*, p.150ff.

9 For general information about Indian terra-cottas see *Das Gupta, C.C.*, Origin and Evolution of Indian Clay Sculpture, Calcutta 1961

10 Quoted from *Rāmacandra Kaulācāra*, Silpa Prakāsa (English ed. by A.Boner and S.R.Sarmā). Leyden 1966, p.103 (here translated into German). For the tantrist worship see: *Zannas-Auboyer*, Khajurāho. The Hague 1960

11 Quoted from *H.Goetz* and *R.Ilse-Munk*, Gedichte aus der

indischen Liebesmystik des Mittelalters (Krishna and Rādhā). Leipzig 1925, p. 55.

12 *Meyer, J.J.*, Das Weib im Altindischen Epos, p. 199

13 *Zimmer, H.*, The Art of Indian Asia. Pantheon Books, vol. I, New York 1955, p. 129

14 *Raghuvamsha* IX, 67; XIII, 49. Meghaduta II, 32

15 *Meyer, J.J.*, Dandin's Dacakumāracaritam. Leipzig 1902, p. 174

16 *Chanda, M.*, "Cosmetic and Coiffure", in: Journal of the Indian Society of Oriental Art, vol. VIII, 1940, pp. 80, 105, 124, 132

17 *Van Lohuizen de Leeuw, J.E.*, Indische Skulpturen der Sammlung Eduard von der Heydt, Rietberg Museum, Zurich 1964, p. 121

18 For example Mahābhārata III, 112, 10 and V, 90, 63

19 *Meyer, J.J.*, Dacakumāracaritam. Leipzig 1902, p. 290f.

20 Bhāgavata Purāna, VIII, 12, 16ff.

21 *Waldschmidt, E.* and *R.L.*, Musikinspirierte Miniaturen. Part I, Wiesbaden 1966, containing a bibliography of the most important literature on Indian miniature painting.

22 *Gangoly, O.C.*, Rāgas and Rāginīs, Bombay 1948; quoted by *L. Hajek*, Indische Miniaturen der Lokalen Schulen, Prague 1961, p. 48

23 *Havell, E.B.*, The Ideals of Indian Art. London 1911, chapter VI, "The Feminine Ideal", p. 89ff.

24 *Meyer, J.J.*, Dacakumāracaritam. Leipzig 1902, p. 142, note 5

25 *Sivaramamurti, C.*, l.c. p. 39, "Dohada". Mālavikāgnimitra III, 12; and Meghaduta II, 17, etc.

26 Agnipurānam, ed. by Manmatha Nath (M.N.) *Dutt*, Calcutta 1913, p. 707

27 Rāmāyana, V, 7, 6 and Raghuvamsha, XVI, 17

28 *Lohuizen de Leeuw*, l.c., p. 100ff.

29 *Sivaramamurti*, l.c., p. 4. Raghuvamsha VI, 23 and XVI, 20

30 See *Saunders, V.*, "Portrait Painting as a Dramatic Devise in Sanskrit Plays", in: Journal of the American Oriental Society, vol. 39, 1919; *Coomaraswamy, A.K.*, "The Traditional Conception of Ideal Portraiture" in: Journal of Indian Society of Oriental Art, 7, 1939

31 *Aravamuthan, T.G.*, Portrait Sculpture in South India. London 1931; *Ghose, A.*, "Some unpublished Early Cola Portrait Sculptures" in: Ostasiatische Zeitschrift, 19, 1953; *Heras, H.*, "The Royal Portraits of Mahabalipuram", in: Acta Orientalia, vol. XIII, 1935

32 *Kramrich, S.*, Grundzüge…, p. 41

33 *Meyer, J.J.*, Dacakumāracaritam, p. 196, note 2

34 *Meyer, J.J.*, Das Weib im Altindischen Epos, p. 250f. Mahābhārata III, 45, 46

35 *Meyer, J.J.*, Das Weib im Altindischen Epos, p. 321/22

36 *Meyer, J.J.*, Das Weib im Altindischen Epos, p. 322

37 *Bhattacharyya, T.*, The Canons of Indian Art, a Study on Vāstuvidyā. Calcutta 1963, 2nd ed., p. 323. Vishnudharmottaram, chapters II and XXXV. Mention must be made here of the above-quoted work by Rāmacandra Kaulācāra, Silpa Prakāsa, Leyden 1966

38 *Bhattacharyya, T.*, l.c., p. 369

39 *Ashraf, K.M.*, Life and Conditions of the People of Hindustan. Delhi 1958, p. 183. Abu'l Fazl is the author of Ain-i-Akbari, the history of Akbar, the great Mogul ruler.

40 For further references about Indian theory of art see *Bhattacharyya, T.*, l.c., p. 101ff.

GLOSSARY

Āgama	Rules on art and literature contained in the Indian scriptures (literally: creeper ornament on vertical panels)
Agnipurānam	The eighth of eighteen great "old" collections of stories called "purānas"
Aindrī (Indrānī)	Goddess, wife of Indra
Amarushataka	Erotic verses ascribed to Amura, 7th or 8th century A.D.
Ānjana	Lampblack
Apsarās	Celestial women dancers, usually dancing at the court of the god Indra
Ardhanā-reshara	Symbol of the union of a god with his shakti
Ardhanārī	The god Shiva represented as half man, half woman
Ashoka	Famous king of the Maurya epoch, 3rd century B.C., supporter of Buddhism
Ashoka tree	Indian tree with beautiful red blossoms
Atibhanga	Woman's pose with one hip vaulted outward
Bhāgavata Purāna	The fifth purāna (see "agnipurānam")
Bhanga	Pose with the body bent
Bhāva-yojanā	Image of moods, shaped to produce rāsa
Bilāval	One of the rāgas (see "rāgamālā")
Brahma	First of the three chief Hindu deities (Brahma, Vishnu, Shiva)
Cakora	Partridge-like bird, supposed to feed on the rays of the moon
Cāmundā	One of the appearances of Shiva's wife
Candī	Like Cāmundā appearance of Shiva's wife in one of her cruel shapes
Chaitya	Shrine, sanctuary, temple-hall
Citra	Term of Indian theory of art, chiefly used for painting
Dampati	Married couple; like mithuna a term used for couples of lovers in Indian art
Dānavī	Female demons, enemies of gods
Dashakumāra-caritam	The stories of the ten princes; a famous work of fiction by the poet Dandin (about A.D. 800)
Devasundarī	A beautiful deity; like sūrasundarī a term used for those deities who have no precise name
Devatā	Deity
Dharmashās-tras	Standard Hindu work in verse on dharma (religion, law, morals and behaviour)
Dohada	Passionate desire, lust; the dohada of plants consists in their irresistable desire to be touched by a beautiful maiden's foot etc., which would further the growth of flowers
Draupadi	Wife of the five Pāndavas, the heroes of the Indian epic Mahābhārata
Durgā	One of the names of Shiva's wife
Ganas	Host of demi-gods in the escort of Indra (or Shiva); usually shown as dwarfs
Gandharvas	Demi-gods, celestial musicians
Ganesha	God with an elephant's head, chief of the ganas, son of Shiva
Gangā	River-goddess (Ganges)
Ganikā	Prostitute (courtesan) living in town

Gopīs	Shepherdesses, milkmaids; playmates of young Krishna
Gunas	Virtues, characteristics of human behaviour
Guru	Hindu spiritual teacher
Himavat	Himālaya
Holi	Indian spring festival
Indra	Aryan god; chief of the Vedic gods
Indrāni	Wife of Indra
Jainism	Religion of a non-Brahmanical sect with doctrine similar to that of Buddhism; founded about 500 B.C. by Mahāvīra (see "Mahāvīra")
Jātakas	Collection of stories about Buddha's re-birth
Kakubha	One of the rāgas (see "rāgamālā")
Kālī	Appearance of Shiva's wife in one of her cruel shapes
Kalpavriksha	Mythical tree with the power to grant wishes
Kāma	God of love; desire
Kāmabandha, Kāmakalā	Love-imagery
Kāmasūtra	"Manual of love" by Vātsyāyana, approximately 4th–6th centuries A.D.
Kanthasutra embrace	A special kind of embrace
Kārttikeya	God of war, son of Shiva
Kinnaris	Demi-gods, often in the shape of birds
Krishna	Indian god of the shepherds; 8th incarnation of Vishnu
Kumāh Rāga	One of the rāgas ("jug-rāga"), (see rāgamalā")
Lakshmī	Goddess of fortune, sometimes called Shrī; wife of Vishnu
Lāvanya yojanā	The creation of beauty, a basic notion of the Indian theory of art
Linga	Phallus, symbol of Shiva
Madhyā	Half bashful, half bold nāyikā
Mahābhārata	Famous Indian heroic epic, approximately 400 B.C., final version 4th–6th centuries A.D.
Mahādevī	The Great Goddess, one of the names of Durgā, Shiva's wife
Mahāvīra	Founder of Jainism, contemporary of Buddha
Mahā-vīryā	Wife of the sun-god Sūrya
Makara	Vāhana and symbol of the river-goddess Gangā, a hybrid being with head of a crocodile
Mālinī	Gardener or flower woman
Manasā	Snake-goddess
Mārā	A demon, the Buddhist satan
Mātrikas	Mother-goddesses; their number is given sometimes as seven or eight, sometimes as sixteen
Māyā	Mother of Buddha
Mithuna	Couple of lovers
Moksha	Release from existence in the world and from transmigration; liberation
Mudrā	Gestures as symbols of moods, attitude of the limbs
Mugdhā	A bashful nāyikā
Nāgarāja	King of snakes
Nāginis	Snake-goddesses, female demons
Nāyaka	Hero or male partner of heroine in Indian erotic literature
Nāyikā	Heroine or female partner of a hero in Indian erotic literature
Pārvatī	One of the names of Shiva's wife
Payas	Milk or water, part of the cloud-symbol for the milk-giving woman's breast
Pramānas	Measures and proportions as source of reliable knowledge; notion of Indian theory of art
Praudhā	A bold nāyikā
Pūja	Worship, sacrifice
Purānas	Sacred books of Hinduism, collection of old stories and legends, approximately 4th–6th centuries A.D.
Rādhā	Shepherdess, beloved of Krishna
Rāga hindola	Rāga on a swing (see "rāgamālā")
Rāgamālā	Literally "garlands of melodies", a collection of main, secondary and subsidiary melody-pictures, called rāga (male) and rāginī (female) respectively
Raghuvamsha	Epic by Kalidasa (5th century A.D.), the most outstanding among the poets of Indian classic literature
Rāginī Bhairavī	Rāginī on way to temple
Rāginī Vasanta	Spring melody
Rājas (raja-king)	Attitude symbolizing might and force
Rākshasis	Female demon
Rāma	Hero of the Indian epic Rāmāyana, one of the purānas
Rāsa	Literally taste or flavour, juice, sweetness: basic notion of beauty in Indian art and eroticism
Rasikapriyā	Theory of love by Keshavadās Mishra (1555 to 1617)
Ratha	Literally: chariot; temple carved out of living rock and then standing free, detached from it
Rishis	Legendary seers, composers of Vedic hymns, later name used for "holy men"
Rupabheda	Technical term of the Indian theory of art for the differentiation of shape
Sadrishya	Likeness or true observation, a technical term of the Indian theory of art
Samyoga	Happy love, sexual consummation
Sarasvatī	Wife of Brahma; originally probably a river-goddess, later the goddess of speech and learning
Sashthī	Goddess of childbirth
Sāttva	Expression of contemplation and poise
Savarnā	Wife of the sun-god Sūrya
Shadanga	The six essentials ("limbs") of the Indian theory of art as stated by Yasodhara in his commentary to the Kāmasūtra (Gupta period)
Shakti	Active and creative power of a god; his feminine complement personified by his wife
Shilpa Prakāsha	Manual of art by Kaulācāra
Shiva	The third of the three chief Hindu deities (Brahma, Vishnu, Shiva)
Shrī	See "Lakshmi"
Shringāra	Emotions, feelings
Sitā	Heroine of the epic Rāmāyana, wife of Rāma
Sitalā	Goddess of smallpox

Stambhaput-talikā	Maiden at a pillar; term used in Indian literature, applied to images of certain women supporting themselves at a pillar
Stūpa	Shrine for sacred relics, monumental Buddhist or Jain building
Sūrasundarī	See "Devasundarī"
Sūrya	Sun-god
Svātī	Wife of Sūrya
Tāmas	Attitude expressing destructive and bellicose activity
Tantric cults	A form of Indian worship connected with magic
Theravāda	Doctrine of the Southern Buddhist School (formerly often called "Hinayāna"), a sect formed soon after Buddha's death
Torana	Gateway; usually leading to the stūpa of old Buddhist buildings
Tribhanga	Attitude formed by a threefold bend of the body
Tvashtri	The Divine Creator; in the Rigveda called the "divine craftsman"
Umā	One of the names of Shiva's wife
Urvashi	Celestial nymph
Utkā	Nāyikā, a maiden waiting at night in the country for her lover
Vāhana	Vehicle or seat, an attribute of a god, or an animal accompanying him
Varnika-bhanga	Differentiation of colours; term of Indian theory of art
Vātsyāyana	Author of Kāmasūtra
Veshyā	Courtesan living in town
Vidhyādharis	Demi-gods, magicians
Vinā	The most ancient string instrument, sometimes plucked with a plectrum like a lute
Vipralabdhā	Nāyikā waiting at night in vain for her lover
Virāha	Unhappy love, separation of lovers
Vishnu	Second of the three main Hindu deities (Brahma, Vishnu, Shiva)
Vishnudhar-mottara	Oldest Indian theoretical treatise on art (Gupta period)
Vrikshakās	Tree-goddesses, dryads
Yaksha (f. yakshi or yakshinī)	Demi-god, protective nature spirit, demon
Yama	God of death, ruler of the realm of the dead
Yamunā	River-goddess (Jumna)
Yogini	Initiate in yoga
Yoni	Symbol of female sex; vulva

CHRONOLOGICAL TABLE

Harappa civilization *Mohenjo Daro; Harappa*	3rd and 2nd millennium B.C.
Old Buddhist art or Shunga, Gandhāra, Kushāna and Āndhara periods *Amarāvatī, Bhārhut; Bodh Gayā; Kanheri; Kārla; Mathurā; Nāgārjunakonda; Sānchī*	1st century B.C. to 3rd century A.D.
Classical art or Gupta period *Ahichhatra; Aihole; Ajantā; Panna*	4th–6th centuries
Art of early Middle Ages *Aurangabad; Elephanta; Ellora; Mahābalipuram*	7th–8th centuries
Art of high Middle Ages *Belur; Bhuvaneshvara; Chidambaram; Khajurāho; Konarak*	9th–13th centuries
Mogul art	16th–18th centuries
Rājasthān and Pahari miniatures *Bundi; Kāngrā; Kishangar; Kotah; Mārwār*	17th–18th centuries
Popular art	19th and 20th centuries
Modern painting	20th century

Site of the main places mentioned in this book; the frontier between India and Pakistan is not shown.

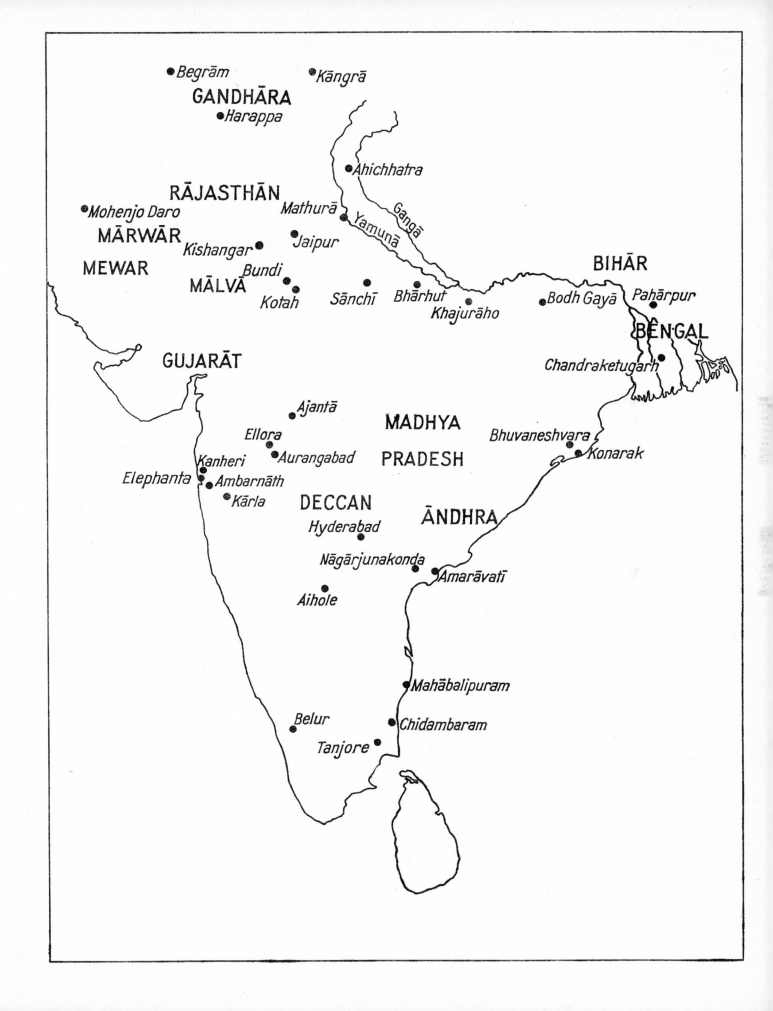

- Begrām
- Kāngrā

GANDHĀRA

- Harappa

- Ahichhatra

RĀJASTHĀN

- Mohenjo Daro
- Mathurā
- Yamunā
- Gangā

MĀRWĀR

- Kishangar
- Jaipur

MEWAR

BIHĀR

- Bundi

MĀLVĀ

- Kotah
- Sānchī
- Bhārhut
- Khajurāho
- Bodh Gayā
- Pahārpur

BENGAL

GUJARĀT

- Chandraketugarh

- Ajantā

MADHYA

- Bhuvaneshvara

- Ellora
- Aurangabad

PRADESH

- Konarak

- Kanheri
- Elephanta
- Ambarnāth

- Kārla

DECCAN

ĀNDHRA

- Hyderabad

- Nāgārjunakonda
- Amarāvatī

- Aihole

- Mahābalipuram

- Belur
- Chidambaram

- Tanjore

COMMENTS ON ILLUSTRATIONS

ILLUSTRATIONS IN THE TEXT

PLATES

5 *Ganesha with his Wife*
Stone sculpture from the outer wall of a temple. Khajurāho, about A.D. 1000. Khajurāho Museum.

6 *Indrāni*
Stone sculpture in a rock cave, considerably over life-size. Ellora, cave 33, about A.D. 800.

7 *The River-goddess Gangā*
Rock sculpture, over life-size. Ellora, cave 21. Rāmeshvara, approximately 7th–8th centuries

8 *Nāgini*
Stone sculpture on the outer wall of a temple. Height 80 cm. Bhuvaneshvara, about A.D. 1000.

9 *Ardhanāreshvara*
Shiva represented as half man, half woman. Detail of a stone relief from Shiva's rock temple in Elephanta. Height 5.90 m. About A.D. 700.

10 *Nāgarāja with his Wife*
Sculpture carved in the living rock. Height approximately 1.50 m. Ajantā, cave 19, 6th century.

11 *The River-goddess Yamunā*
Terra-cotta, life-size. From Ahichhatra, approximately 5th century. National Museum, Delhi.

12 *Shiva and Pārvati*
Detail of a stone relief. Measurements of the relief 2.45 × 1.35 m. Aihole, about A.D. 600. Prince of Wales Museum, Bombay.

13 *Divine Couple*
Rock sculpture, smaller than life-size. Ajantā, cave 16, 5th century

14 a) *Sirimā Devatā*
Stone pillar of the balustrade of the stūpa, height 2.14 m. Bhārhut, about 100 B.C. Indian Museum, Calcutta.

14 b) *Culakokā Devatā*
Stone pillar of the balustrade of the stūpa, height 2.14 m. Bhārhut, about 100 B.C. Indian Museum, Calcutta.

15 *Vrikshakā*
Sculpture of red sandstone from Mathurā, height 50 cm. About 2nd century. Victoria & Albert Museum, London, Inv. No. I.M. 73–1927.

16 *Vrikshakā*
Stone sculpture on the east gate of stūpa I, at Sānchī; height of gate 10.40 m. 1st century B.C.

17 *Female Dancer in front of a Tree*
Stone sculpture at the outer wall of a temple, set obliquely upon a stone pillar as support of the roof; approximately life-size. Belur, Keshava temple, 12th century.

18 *Yogini under a Tree*
Mogul miniature. Prince of Wales Museum, Bombay, Inv. No. 4329.

19 *Courtesan with Servant in a Garden*
Bundi miniature, late 17th century. Prince of Wales Museum, Bombay, Inv. No. 5592.

20 *Yakshini*
Small terra-cotta sculpture, Chandraketugarh, about 2nd century. Asutosh Museum, Calcutta.

21 *Smallpox Goddess Sitalā*
Over life-size sculpture of clay. Modern popular art of Bengal from a village north of Calcutta.

22 *Durgā killing the Bull-demon*
Alabaster, height 33 cm. Rājasthān, 18th–19th centuries. Collection Heinz Mode.

23 *Krishna's Youth*
Rājasthān miniature. Prince of Wales Museum, Bombay, Inv. No. 5232.

24 *Durgā on a Tiger*
Miniature from a manuscript of Devī Mahatmaya. Gurajāt, 15th century. Prince of Wales Museum, Bombay, Inv. No. 5638.

25 *Jasoda with the Krishna-child*
Bazaar painting in water-colours, measurements 42 × 26 cm. Kālīghāt, Calcutta, about 1880. Collection Heinz Mode.

26 *Woman asking two Yoginis to bless her Child*
Detail of a miniature; measurements of the entire miniature 26.4 × 17.2 cm. Oudh, late 18th century. State Museums, Berlin, Inv. No. J. 4594 fol. 6a.

27 *Mother holding a Child*
Small wood statuette. Burdwan, Bengal. Popular art, 19th century. Asutosh Museum, Calcutta.

28 *Mother with Child*
Black stone. Rajshahi, Bengal, 11th century. Asutosh Museum, Calcutta.

29 *Woman holding a Child*
Stone sculpture on the outer wall of a temple; height 1 m. Khajurāho, about A.D. 1000.

30 a) *Mothers with Children and Women occupied with Domestic Work*
Stone sculpture probably from the outer wall of a temple at Khajurāho. The figures are smaller than life-size. Khajurāho Museum.

30 b) *Reclining Woman with Child*
Detail of a figurative frieze; the figures are smaller than life-size. Probably from the outer wall of the same temple as 30 a. Khajurāho Museum.

31 *Mithuna Couple*
Cut in the living rock, about life-size. Entrance hall to Chaitya cave of Kārla. 1st century A.D.

32 *Mithuna Groups*
Cut in the living rock, about life-size. Entrance hall to Chaitya cave of Kanheri, 2nd century A.D.

33 *Pair of Figures*
Small sculpture of bronze, probably from Gujarāt, about 2nd century A.D. Baroda Museum, Baroda.

34 *Krishna and Rādhā*
The couple of lovers is shown twice in this miniature from Nurpur. Measurements 19 × 27 cm., about 1790. Victoria & Albert Museum, London, Inv. No. I. S. 42–1961.

35 *Couple of Lovers under Trees*
Oil painting by Samant Kar, Calcutta. 50 × 80 cm., 1959. Collection Heinz Mode.

36 *Shiva and Pārvatī*
Stone sculpture on the outer wall of the Pārshvanātha temple, height approximately 1 m. Khajurāho, about A.D. 1000.

37 *Couple of Lovers*
Stone sculpture on the outer wall of the Devī Jagadambā temple, height approximately 80 cm. Khajurāho, about A.D. 1000.

38 *Couple of Lovers*
Miniature from a manuscript by Amarushataka (Mālvā School). Measurements 21×15 cm., about 1680. Prince of Wales Museum, Bombay.

39 *Love in the Rain (Krishna and Rādhā)*
Miniature, Bundi School. 17th–18th centuries. Prince of Wales Museum, Bombay, Inv. No. 5569.

40 *Pair of Figures and Man on Elephant*
On the outer wall of a ratha, a temple carved out of the living rock to stand as a detached building. Height about 1.50 m. Arjuna Ratha at Mahābalipuram, 7th–8th centuries.

41 *Couple of Lovers*
Stone sculpture on the outer wall of the Devī Jagadambā temple, height about 80 cm. Khajurāho, about A.D. 1000.

42 *Couple of Lovers*
Stone sculpture on the outer wall of the Temple of the Sun at Konarak; a bit smaller than life-size. About A.D. 1250.

43 *Couple of Lovers*
Wood, probably originally a decoration on the outside of a building; height about 1 m. Gujarāt, popular art, 18th century (?) Collection Purohit, Bombay.

44 *Couple of Lovers*
Stone sculpture on the outer wall of the temple, smaller than life-size. Konarak, about A.D. 1250.

45 *Woman adorned for Festive Occasion*
Krishna and Rādhā surrounded by Rādhā's fellow shepherdesses. Miniature of the Bundi School. Prince of Wales Museum, Bombay.

46 *Queen going for a Walk accompanied by her Servants*
Detail of a mural painting on the surface of rock. Ajantā, cave 17, early 6th century.

47 *Royal Couple*
Detail of a mural painting on the wall of a rock cave. Ajantā, cave 17, early 6th century.

48 *Woman with Fly-whisk and Censer*
Grey marble, height 1 m. South-east Rājasthān or west Madhya Pradesh, 11th–12th centuries. Rietberg Museum, Zurich, Inv. No. RVJ 202.

49 *a) Woman with Servants*
Wood carving, height approximately 30 cm. Bengal popular art, about 1800. Gurusaday Museum, near Calcutta.

49 *b) Lamenting Women and Women on a Journey*
Wood carving, height approximately 30 cm. Bengal popular art, about 1800. Gurusaday Museum, near Calcutta.

50 *Woman with Small Vessel*
Fragment of a stone sculpture from the outer wall of a temple; smaller than life-size. Khajurāho, Khajurāho Museum.

51 *Woman carrying a Sword*
Stone sculpture on the outer wall of the Kandāriya temple, height approximately 1 m. Khajurāho, about A.D. 1000.

52 *Ladies with Servants on the Terrace of a Palace*
Bundi miniature, measurements 21×31 cm. About 1780. Victoria & Albert Museum, London, Inv. No. I.S. 96–1952.

53 *Women at the Village Well*
Miniature of the Mogul School, measurements 19×27 cm. About 1720. Victoria & Albert Museum, London, Inv. No. I. S. 42–1961.

54 *Woman carrying a Whisk (Yakshinī)*
Smoothly polished stone, height 1.20 m. Didarganj Museum, 1st-2nd centuries A.D.

55 *Servant*
Ivory carving, height 11 cm. Begrām, 2nd century A.D. Kabul Museum.

56 *Women on a Visit to Holy Men, leaving a Cart drawn by Oxen*
Detail of a miniature, Bundi School, 18th century. Prince of Wales Museum, Bombay, Inv. No. 5365.

57 *Woman milking a Cow*
Miniature, Rāgaputra. Measurements 13.5×18.3 cm. From Bilaspur, about 1750. State Museums of Prussian Properties of Works of Art, Berlin-Dahlem, Inv. No. I 5579².

58 *Women playing Polo*
Miniature, Mogul School, late 17th century. Prince of Wales Museum, Bombay, Inv. No. 15319.

59 *Chānd Bībī hunting with a Falcon*
The queen-dowager of Bijapur, born princess of Ahmednagar which she defended against attacks by the Moguls; end of 16th century. Miniature, Deccan School, Hyderabad, 18th century. Prince of Wales Museum, Bombay, Inv. No. 223440.

60 *Noble Women smoking the Hookah*
Miniature, Bundi School, 18th century. Prince of Wales Museum, Bombay, Inv. No. 5290.

61 *Woman devoutly folding her Hands*
Detail of a group of life-size stone sculptures inside a cave in the rock. Aurangabad, 7th century.

62 *Praying Women*
Detail of the group mentioned under No. 61. Aurangabad, 7th century.

63 *Women mourning at the Mahāparinirvāna, the Death of Buddha*
Detail of a huge rock sculpture. Ajantā, cave 26, 7th century.

64 *Woman painting the Soles of her Feet*
Stone sculpture on the outer wall of the Pārshvanātha temple, height approximately 1 m. Khajurāho, about A.D. 1000.

65 *Woman holding a Mirror*
Stone sculpture on the outer wall of the Kandāriya

temple, height approximately 1 m. Khajurāho, about A.D. 1000.

66 *Woman with Paint-brush for Eyes*
Stone sculpture on the outer wall of the Pārshvanātha temple, height 1 m. Khajurāho, about A.D. 1000.

67 *Woman dressing*
Stone sculpture on the outer wall of the Pārshvanātha temple, height approximately 1 m. Khajurāho, about A.D. 1000.

68 *Woman extracting a Thorn from her Foot*
Stone sculpture on the outer wall of the Kandāriya temple, height approximately 1 m. Khajurāho, about A.D. 1000.

69 *Krishna and the bathing Shepherdesses*
Miniature; measurements 30×21 cm. Mārwār, second half of 18th century. Prince of Wales Museum, Bombay, Inv. No. 5223.

70 *Playing in the Water (Krishna and Gopīs)*
Detail of a miniature, Mewar. Prince of Wales Museum. Bombay.

71 *Bathing Women*
Detail of a miniature; Kotah (Bundi School), 18th century. Prince of Wales Museum, Bombay, Inv. No. 5718/2.

72 *Lady dressing her Hair*
Miniature of Kangra School; measurements 13×17.5 cm. About 1800. Victoria & Albert Museum, London, Inv. No. I. S. 122–1960.

73 *Squatting Woman adorning herself*
Bazaar painting in water colours. Kālīghāt, Calcutta. Late 19th century. Private collection, London.

74 *Lady with Love-letter*
Miniature, Oudh, mid 18th century. Measurements 19×10.8 cm. State Museums, Berlin, Inv. No. J. 4591 fol. 15a.

75 *Lady with Flower*
Bazaar painting in water colours, 19th century. Private collection, London.

76 *Temple Wall with Vrikshakās*
Stone sculptures at Bhuvaneshvara, smaller than life-size. Approximately 11th century.

77 *Dancers*
Small terra-cotta sculpture, Pahārpur, Bengal. Asutosh Museum, Calcutta.

78 *Woman with Mirror*
Stone sculpture at the outer wall of the Keshava temple set obliquely upon a stone pillar as support of the roof; about life-size. Belur, 12th century.

79 *Woman Musician*
Stone sculpture at the outer wall, just below the roof of the Keshava temple; approximately life-size. Belur, 12th century.

80 *Woman playing the Flute*
Stone sculpture at the outer wall of the Keshava temple set obliquely upon a stone pillar as support of the roof; about life-size. Belur, 12th century.

81 *Female Dancer*
Stone sculpture at the outer wall, just below the roof, of the Keshava temple; about life-size. Belur, 12th century.

82 *Female Dancer*
Bronze, height 10 cm. Mohenjo Daro, 3rd millennium B.C.

83 *Women Dancers and Musicians*
Marble. Ceiling of the Jain temple. Dilvara, 12th century.

84 *Woman Dancer and Musicians*
Stone sculpture on the wall of the Nateshvara-Shiva temple, smaller than life-size. Chidambaram, South India, 16th century.

85 *Madhu Mālavī Rāginī*
Miniature; Mārwār, 17th century. Prince of Wales Museum, Bombay, Inv. No. 391.

86 *Maidens on a Swing*
Miniature; Sorapur. Prince of Wales Museum, Bombay, Inv. No. 4317.

87 *Dancing Maidens*
Miniature, Deccan School, Hyderabad. Prince of Wales Museum, Bombay, Inv. No. 4357.

88 *Woman with Bird*
Stone sculpture at the outer wall of the Keshava temple, set obliquely upon a stone pillar as support of the roof; about life-size. Belur, 12th century.

89 *Woman with Plants and Animals*
Stone sculpture on the outer wall of a temple, height approximately 80 cm. Bhuvaneshvara, about A.D. 1000.

90 *"La Belle et la bête"*
Brownish sandstone, height 58 cm. West Madhya Pradesh, south-east Rājasthān or north Gujarāt, 10th–11th centuries. Rietberg Museum, Zurich, Inv. No. RVJ 101.

91 *"La Belle et la bête"*
Wood painted in colour, height 58 cm. North Gujarāt, late 16th or 17th century. Rietberg Museum, Zurich, Inv. No. RVJ 401.

92 *Nymph with Scorpion*
Black basalt, height 30 cm. Probably Bihar, second half of 11th or 12th century. Rietberg Museum, Zurich, Inv. No. RVJ 205.

93 *Bathing Woman, Cakora and Ascetic*
White marble, height 73 cm. North Gujarāt or south Rājasthān, 15th century. Rietberg Museum, Zurich, Inv. No. RVJ 208.

94 *Woman at the Door*
Stone sculpture, height about 1 m. Bhuvaneshvara, Baitala-Deo temple, 9th century.

95 *Woman at the Door*
Terra-cotta sculpture on the outer wall of a terra-cotta temple, about life-size. Suri, Bengal, 18th century.

96 *Woman on the so-called Delivery-chair*
Stone sculpture, on top of a temple gate, height 50 cm. Bhuvaneshvara.

97 *Woman chasing a Cat*
Miniature, Bundi School. First half of 18th century. Prince of Wales Museum, Bombay, Inv. No. 5392.

98 *Portrait of a Lady on a Garden Terrace*
Miniature. State Museums, Berlin, Inv. No. 4591, fol. 10.

99 *Lady with Falcon*
Miniature. Guler, measurements 20.5×11 cm. About 1765. Victoria & Albert Museum, London, Inv. No. I.S. 178–1950.

100 *Lady playing the Vīna, and Pair of Antelopes*
Miniature. Kulu, measurements 15×21.8 cm. About 1720. Victoria & Albert Museum, London, Inv. No. I. S. 24–1949.

101 *Portrait of Bahu Begam*
Miniature in the style of Mihr Chand, son of Ganga Ram. Painted between 1775 and 1782. Measurements 21.3×12.9 cm. State Museums, Berlin, Inv. No. J.4594 fol. 8a.

102 *Head of a Woman*
Terra-cotta sculpture, height 22 cm. Panna, Bengal. About 5th century. Asutosh Museum, Calcutta.

103 *Buddha taming an Elephant which had run wild*
Stone medallion from the railings of the stūpa of Amarāvatī. Diameter 1.07 cm. 2nd century A.D.

104 *Woman seen in Profile*
Over life-size stone figure. Konarak, Temple of the Sun, about A.D. 1250.

105 *Sūrasundarī*
Stone sculpture from the outer wall of the Temple of the Sun; approximately life-size. Konarak, about A.D. 1250. Birla Academy of Art and Culture, Calcutta.

106 *Maiden (Mugdhā), bashfully covering her Face*
Stone sculpture on the outer wall of the Kandāriya temple; height approximately 1 m. Khajurāho, about A.D. 1000.

107 *Sūrasundarī*
Stone sculpture on the outer wall of the Kandāriya temple; height approximately 1 m. Khajurāho, about A.D. 1000.

108 *Sūrasundarī*
Stone sculpture on the outer wall of the Kandāriya temple; height approximately 1 m. Khajurāho, about A.D. 1000.

109 *Woman holding a Vessel*
Stone sculpture on the outer wall of the Kandāriya temple; height approximately 1 m. Khajurāho, about A.D. 1000.

110 *Figures of Women on a Temple Wall*
Stone sculpture, about life-size. Ambarnath temple, 11th century.

111 *Woman standing on a Pedestal representing a Lotus*
Stone sculpture on the outer wall of the Rājarāni temple; height 80 cm. Bhuvaneshvara, 12th century.

112 *Sūrasundarī*
Stone sculpture from the outer wall of a temple; height approximately 1 m. Khajurāho. Khajurāho Museum.

113 *Female Nude*
Pink sandstone, height 38 cm. Rājasthān, north Gujarāt or west Madhya Pradesh, 10th or 11th century. Rietberg Museum, Zurich, Inv. No. RVJ 108.

114 *Sitting Woman*
Wood carving, height approximately 1 m. Bengal, popular art, about 1800. Gurusaday Museum, near Calcutta.

115 *Prince meeting his Beloved at Night*
Miniature, Bundi School. Prince of Wales Museum, Bombay, Inv. No. 5590.

116 *Clandestine Meeting of Lovers*
Miniature, Bundi School, 18th century. Prince of Wales Museum, Bombay, Inv. No. 5386.

117 *Sorrows of Separation*
Miniature, Bundi School. Prince of Wales Museum, Bombay, Inv. No. 5313.

118 *Unconscious Heroine surrounded by her Servants and Friends*
Miniature, Kangra School, 18th century. Prince of Wales Museum, Bombay, Inv. No. 558.

SOURCES
OF ILLUSTRATIONS

BAAC, Calcutta: 105
Baroda Museum, Baroda: 33
Birnbaum, Halle: 22, 35
Chandra, Bombay: 3, 5–10, 12, 13, 16–19, 23, 24, 29–31, 36–42, 44, 45, 50, 51, 56, 58–71, 79–81, 83, 85–89, 97, 104, 106–112, 115–118
Department of Archaeology of India, Delhi: 11, 14, 54, 94
Government Museum, Madras: 103
Guha, Calcutta: 20, 27, 28, 77, 102
Hansmann, Munich, 15, 34, 52, 53, 72, 73, 75, 99, 100
Kabul Museum, Kabul: 55
Mode, Halle: 21, 43, 49, 84, 95, 96, 114
Peuke, Halle: 32
Püschel, Halle (Photograph of plaster cast): 82
Rapho, Paris: 76
Rietberg Museum, Zurich: 4, 48, 90–93, 113
State Museums, Berlin: 26
State Museums of Prussian Properties of Works of Art, Berlin-Dahlem: 57
UNESCO: 46, 47
Verlag der Kunst, Dresden (Frewel, Potsdam): 74, 98, 101

We wish to thank the following Museums and Institutions for the permission to reproduce items of their collections:

Asutosh Museum, Calcutta: 20, 27, 28, 77, 104
Birla Academy of Art and Culture, Calcutta: 105
Gurusaday Museum, near Calcutta: 49, 116
Indian Museum, Calcutta: 14
Khajurāho Museum, Khajurāho: 5, 30, 50, 114
National Museum, Delhi: 11
Prince of Wales Museum, Bombay: 12, 18, 19, 23, 24, 38, 39, 45, 56, 58, 59, 60, 69, 70, 71, 85, 86, 87, 97, 118–120
Purohit Collection, Bombay: 43
State Museums, Berlin: 26, 74, 98, 101
State Museums of Prussian Properties of Works of Art, Berlin-Dahlem: 57
Victoria & Albert Museum, London: 15, 34, 52, 53, 72, 73, 100

PLATES

Pārvatī (?)

3

7

10 *Nāgarāja with his Wife*

11   *The River-goddess Yamunā*

Divine Couple

Courtesan with Servant in a Garden

Durgā on a Tiger 24

25 *Jasoda with the Krishna-child*

Couple of Lovers under Trees

35

Couple of Lovers

39   *Love in the Rain (Krishna and Rādhā)*

40   *Pair of Figures and Man on Elephant*
41   *Couple of Lovers*

45 *Women adorned for Festive Occasion*

46 *Queen going for a Walk accompanied by her Servants*
47 *Royal Couple*

47

Chānd Bibī hunting with a Falcon

67   *Woman dressing*

Krishna and the bathing Shepherdesses

Playing in the Water (Krishna and Gopis) 70

Lady with Flower

Women Dancers and Musicians

Maidens on a Swing

87   *Dancing Maidens*

"La Belle et la bête"

Woman on the so-called Delivery-chair

97   *Woman chasing a Cat*

Lady with Falcon

Portrait of Bahu Begam

Buddha taming an Elephant which had run wild

Maiden (Mugdhā), bashfully covering her Face

Sūrasundarī

Woman holding a Vessel

Woman standing on a Pedestal representing a Lotus

Prince meeting his Beloved at Night